Teach & Test

Reading Grade

Table of Contents

How to Use This Book

1. This book can be used in a home or classroom setting. Read through each unit before working with the student(s). Familiarize yourself with the vocabulary and the skills that are introduced at the top of each unit activity page. Use this information as a guide to help instruct the student(s).

2. Choose a quiet place with little or no interruptions (including the telephone). Talk with the student(s) about the purpose of this book and how you will be working as a team to prepare for standardized tests.

3. As an option, copy the unit test and give it as a pretest to identify weak areas.

4. Upon the completion of each unit, you will find a unit test. Discuss the Helping Hand strategy for test taking featured on the test. Use the example on each test as a chance to show the student(s) how to work through a problem and completely fill in the answer circle. Encourage the student(s) to work independently when possible, but this is a learning time, and questions should be welcomed. A time limit is given for each test. Instruct the student(s) to use the time allowed efficiently, looking back over the answers if possible. Tell him to continue until he sees the stop sign.

5. Record the score on the record sheet on page 4. If a student has difficulty with any questions, use the cross-reference guide on the inside back cover to identify the skills that need to be reviewed.

Teach & Test

Introduction

Now this makes sense—teaching students the skills and strategies that are expected of them before they are tested!

Many students, parents, and teachers are concerned that standardized test scores do not adequately reflect a child's capabilities. This may be due to one or more of the factors italicized below. The purpose of this book is to reduce the negative impact of these, or similar factors, on a student's standardized test scores. The goal is to target those factors and alter their effects as described.

1. *The student has been taught the tested skills but has forgotten them.* This book is divided into units that are organized similarly to first grade textbooks. Instructions for the skill itself are found at the top of each unit activity page, ensuring that the student has been exposed to each key component. The exercises include drill/practice and creative learning activities. Additional activity suggestions can be found in a star burst within the units. These activities require the student to apply the skills that they are practicing.
2. *The student has mastered the skills but has never seen them presented in a test-type format.* Ideally, the skills a student learns at school will be used as part of problem solving in the outside world. For this reason, the skills in this book, and in most classrooms, are not practiced in a test-type format. At the end of each unit in this book, the skills are specifically matched with test questions. In this way, the book serves as a type of "bridge" between the skills that the student(s) has mastered and the standardized test format.
3. *The student is inexperienced with the answer sheet format.* Depending on the standardized test that your school district uses, students are expected to fill in the answer circles completely and neatly. The unit, midway review, and final review tests will help prepare the student(s) for this process.
4. *The student may feel the anxiety of a new and unfamiliar situation.* While testing, students will notice changes in their daily routine: their classroom door will be closed with a "Testing" sign on it, they will be asked not to use the restroom, their desks may be separated, their teacher may read from a script and refuse to repeat herself, etc. To help relieve the stress caused by these changes, treat each unit test in this book as it would be treated at school by following the procedures listed below.

Stage a Test

You will find review tests midway through the book and again at the end of the book. When you reach these points, "stage a test" by creating a real test-taking environment. The procedures listed below coincide with many standardized test directions. The purpose is to alleviate stress, rather than contribute to it, so make this a serious, but calm event and the student(s) will benefit.

1. Prepare! Have the student(s) sharpen two pencils, lay out scratch paper, and use the restroom.
2. Choose a room with a door that can be closed. Ask a student to put a sign on the door that reads "Testing" and explain that no talking will be permitted after the sign is hung.
3. Direct the student(s) to turn to a specific page but not to begin until the instructions are completely given.
4. Read the instructions at the top of the page and work through the example together. Discuss the Helping Hand strategy that is featured at the top of the page. Have the student(s) neatly and completely fill in the bubble for the example. This is the child's last chance to ask for help!
5. Instruct the student(s) to continue working until the stop sign is reached. If a student needs help reading, you may read each question only once.

Helping Hand Test Strategies

The first page of each test features a specific test-taking strategy that will be helpful in working through most standardized tests. These strategies are introduced and spotlighted one at a time so that they will be learned and remembered internally. Each will serve as a valuable test-taking tool, so discuss them thoroughly.

The strategies include:

- Whisper the sounds you are making to yourself.
- Read all the choices before you answer.
- If you are unsure, try each answer in the blank.
- Read carefully and go back to the story if you are unsure.
- Watch for key words in the stories that give you clues.
- Fill in the circles neatly and completely.
- Use your time wisely. If a question seems too tough, skip it and come back to it later.

Constructed-Response Questions

You will find the final question(s) of the tests are written in a different format called constructed response. This means that students are not provided with answer choices, but are instead asked to construct their own answers. The objective of such an "open-ended" type of question is to provide students with a chance to creatively develop reasonable answers. It also provides an insight to a student's reasoning and thinking skills. As this format is becoming more accepted and encouraged by standardized test developers, students will be "ahead of the game" by practicing such responses now.

Evaluating the Tests

Two types of questions are included in each test. The unit tests and the midway review test each consist of 15–20 multiple-choice questions, and the final review test consists of 30 multiple-choice questions. All tests include a constructed-response question which requires the student(s) to construct and sometimes support an answer. Use the following procedures to evaluate a student's performance on each test.

1. Use the answer key found on pages 126–128 to correct the tests. Be sure the student(s) neatly and completely filled in the answer circles.
2. Record the scores on the record sheet found on page 4. If the student(s) incorrectly answered any questions, use the cross-reference guide found on the inside back cover to help identify the skills the student(s) needs to review. Each test question references the corresponding activity page.
3. Scoring the constructed-response questions is somewhat subjective. Discuss these questions with the student(s). Sometimes it is easier for the student(s) to explain the answer verbally. Help the student to record his or her thoughts as a written answer. If the student(s) has difficulty formulating a response, refer back to the activity pages using the cross-reference guide. Also review the star burst activity found in the unit which also requires the student(s) to formulate an answer.
4. Discuss the test with the student(s). What strategies were used to answer the questions? Were some questions more difficult than others? Was there enough time? What strategies did the student(s) use while taking the test?

Record Sheet

Record a student's score for each test by drawing a star or placing a sticker below each item number that was correct. Leave the incorrect boxes empty as this will allow you to visually see any weak spots. Review and practice those missed skills, then retest only the necessary items.

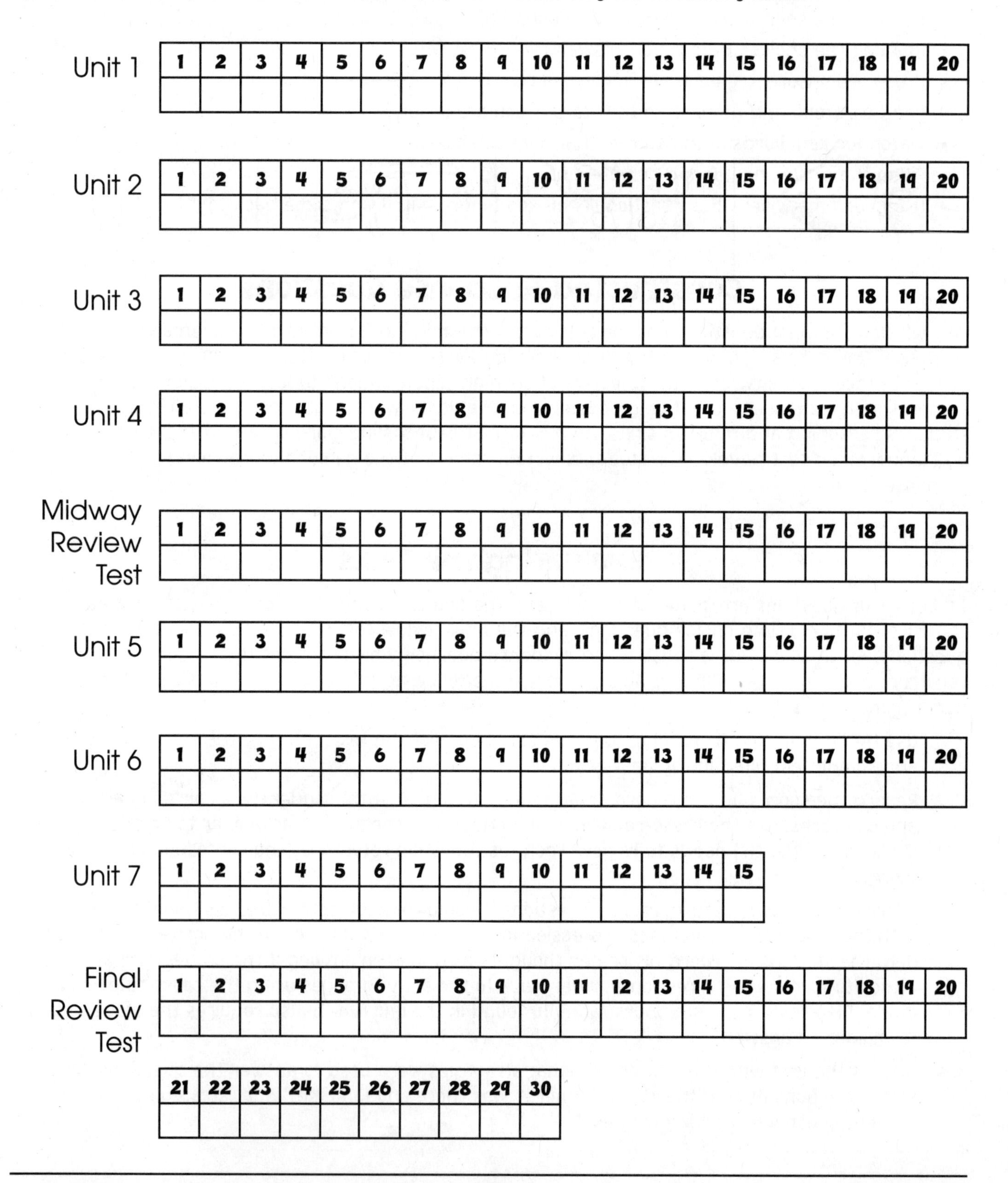

Unit 1	1	2	3	4	5	6	7	8	9	10	11	12	13	14	15	16	17	18	19	20

Unit 2	1	2	3	4	5	6	7	8	9	10	11	12	13	14	15	16	17	18	19	20

Unit 3	1	2	3	4	5	6	7	8	9	10	11	12	13	14	15	16	17	18	19	20

Unit 4	1	2	3	4	5	6	7	8	9	10	11	12	13	14	15	16	17	18	19	20

Midway Review Test	1	2	3	4	5	6	7	8	9	10	11	12	13	14	15	16	17	18	19	20

Unit 5	1	2	3	4	5	6	7	8	9	10	11	12	13	14	15	16	17	18	19	20

Unit 6	1	2	3	4	5	6	7	8	9	10	11	12	13	14	15	16	17	18	19	20

Unit 7	1	2	3	4	5	6	7	8	9	10	11	12	13	14	15

Final Review Test	1	2	3	4	5	6	7	8	9	10	11	12	13	14	15	16	17	18	19	20

21	22	23	24	25	26	27	28	29	30

Name

Letters with one sound

Unit 1

Every word has a beginning sound. It is the first sound the word makes.
The consonant letters b, d, f, h, j, k, l, m, n, p, q, r, t, v, and z make one sound.

Circle the letter that makes the beginning sound of each picture.

1.  v f k	2.  h d b	3.  v r f	4.  z q k
5.  l x j	6.  n m r	7.  k h r	8.  p r d
9.  t l j	10.  x z p	11.  z s x	12.  h r k
13. 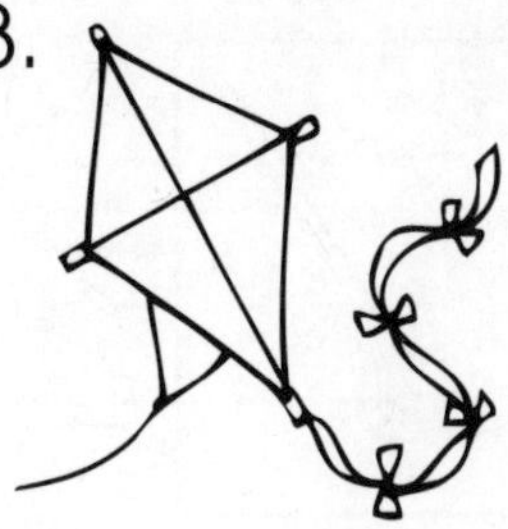 k p b	14. 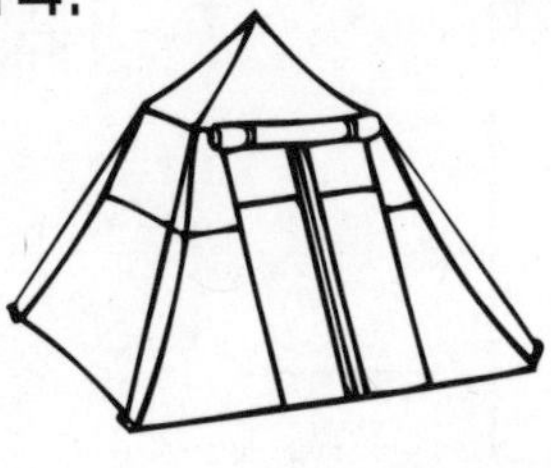 l f t	15.  n m r	16.  b h d

Name

Beginning and ending sounds

Unit 1

All words have a beginning and an ending sound. The **beginning sound** is the first sound you hear. The **ending sound** is the last sound you hear.

Example: dog — The d makes the beginning sound.
The g makes the ending sound.

Write the letter that makes the beginning sound of each picture.

1.  ____

2.  ____

3.  ____

4.  ____

5.  ____

6. 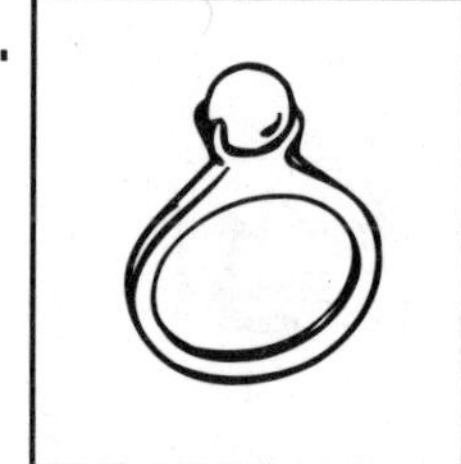 ____

Write the letter that makes the ending sound of each picture.

7. 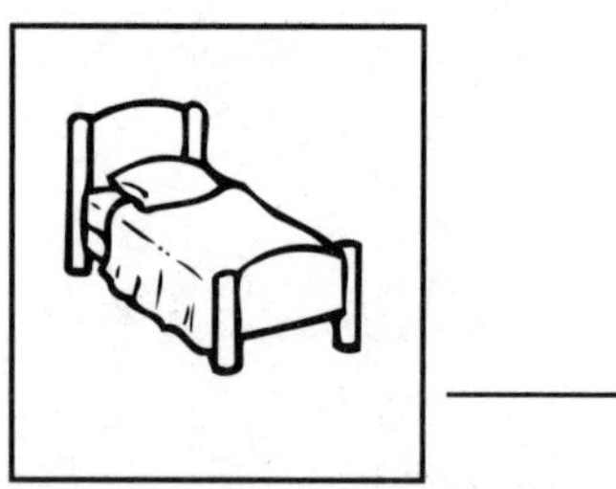 ____

8. 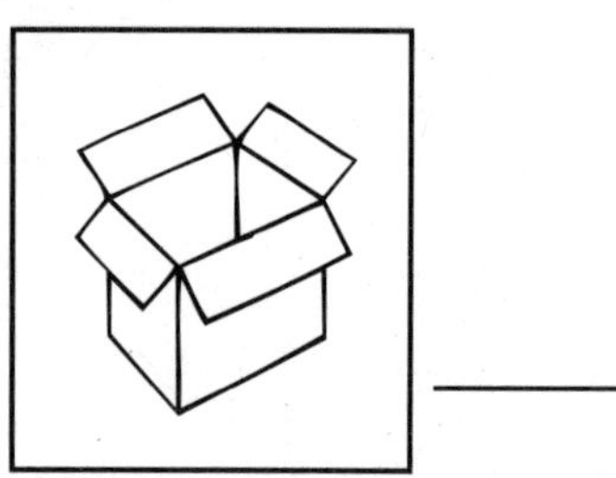 ____

9. 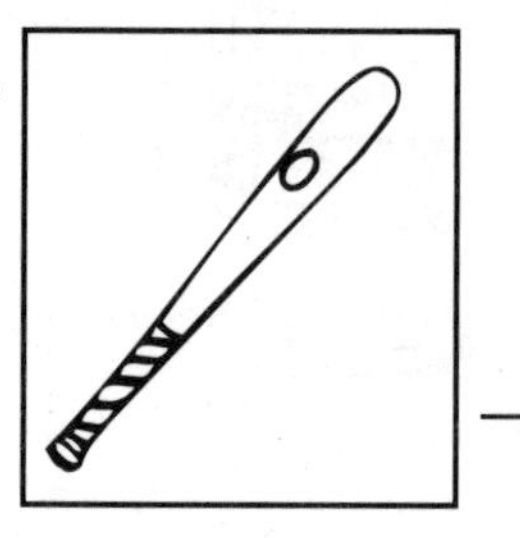 ____

10. 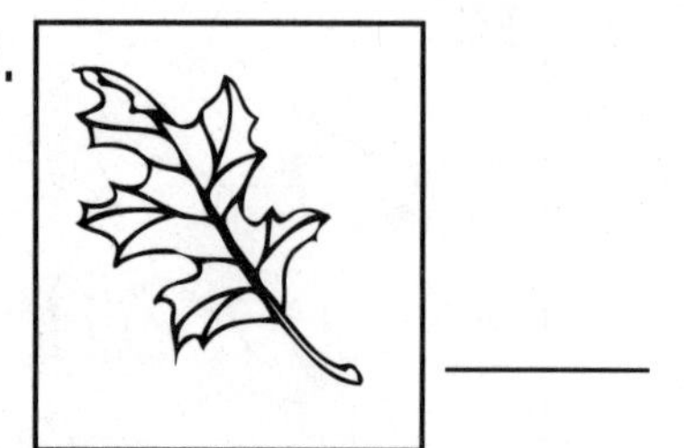 ____

11.  ____

12.  ____

Name

Consonants making more than one sound

Unit 1

Three consonant letters make more than one sound.
They are c, g, and s.
Examples: cat and city, gift and gym, sun and noise

Write a word from the Word Bank below the correct picture.

cow	rose	cent
square	cage	grass
magic	circle	sad

1. 

2. 

3. 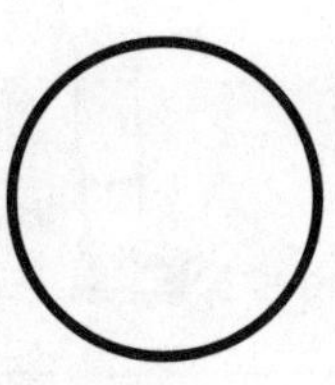

4. 

5. 

6. 

7. 

8. 

9. 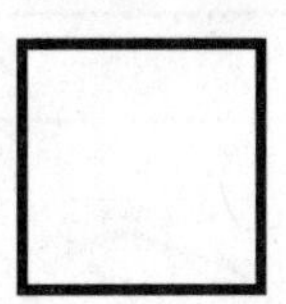

Name

Short vowel sounds

Unit 1

There are five main vowels: a, e, i, o, and u.
The **short vowel sounds** are:

a as in cat   e as in bed   i as in ship   o as in box   u as in tub

Write the middle sound of each word using the correct vowel.

1.  c ___ p

2. 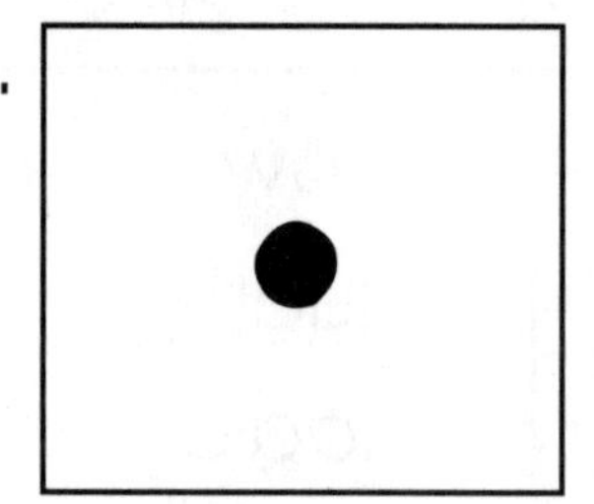 d ___ t

3. 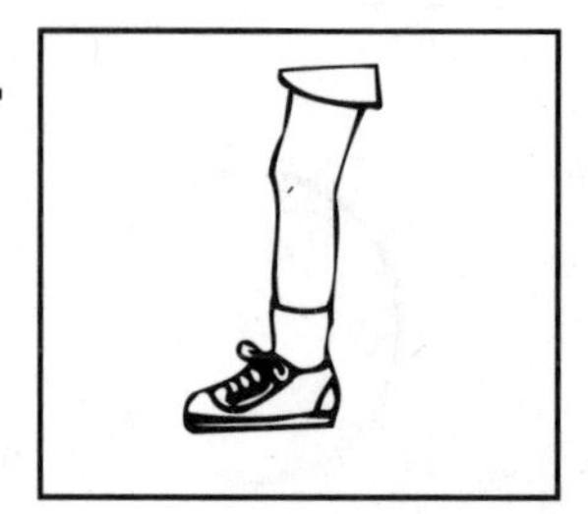 l ___ g

4.  f ___ n

5.  m ___ p

6.  l ___ ps

7.  p ___ g

8.  n ___ t

9.  h ___ t

10.  tr ___ ck

Name

Long vowel sounds

Unit 1

When a vowel sounds like its name, it makes a **long vowel sound**.
Examples: a in take, i in like
When a word has a consonant, vowel, consonant, e pattern (CVCE),
the vowel sound is usually long, and the e is silent.
Examples: name, ride, note, cute

Add the beginning sound and the vowel sound to finish writing each word.

1. 
___ ___ve

2. 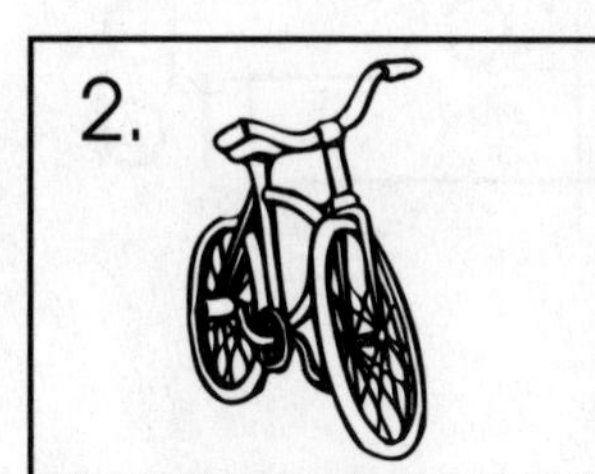
___ ___ke

3. 

___ ___ne

4. 
___ ___me

5. 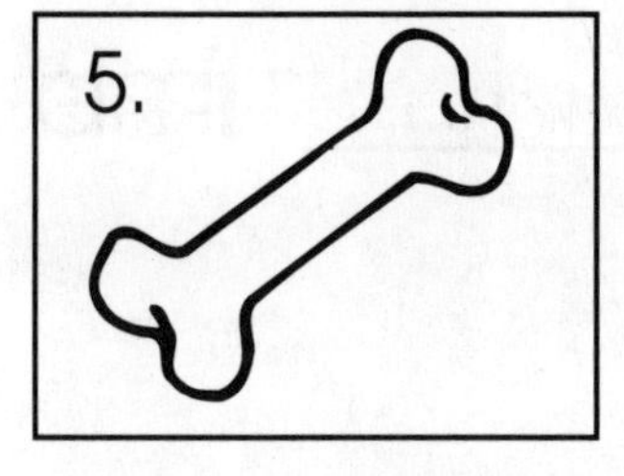
___ ___ne

6. 

___ ___me

7. 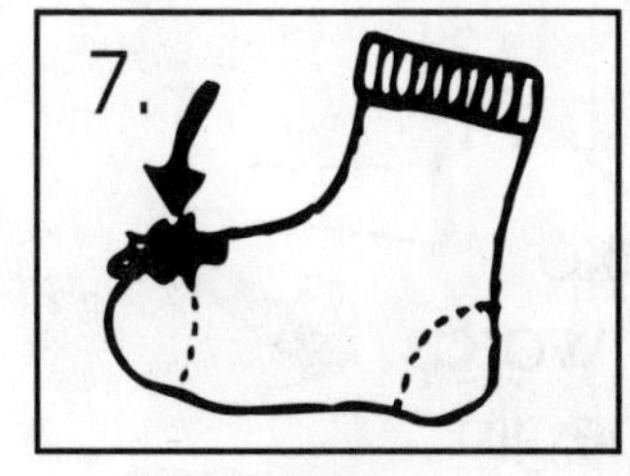
___ ___le

8. 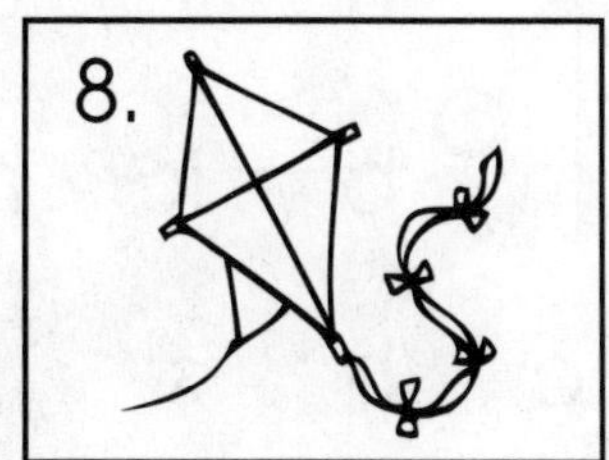
___ ___te

9. 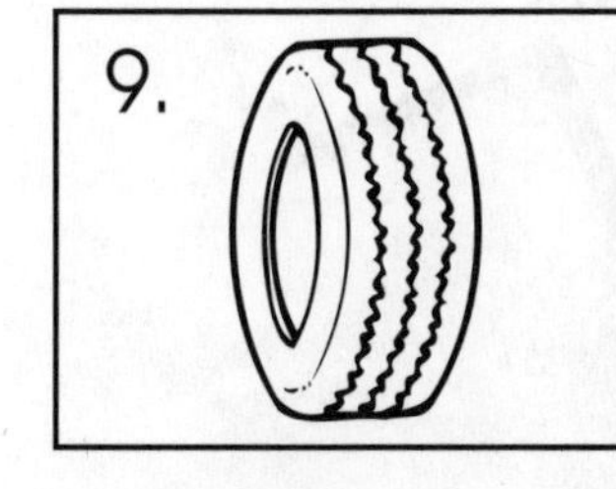
___ ___re

10. 
___ ___ke

Name

Consonant digraphs

Unit 1

When the letters ch, sh, th, and wh come together at the beginning or the ending of a word, they usually make one sound. They are called **consonant digraphs**.

Examples: children, shop, that, when

Add **ch**, **sh**, **th**, or **wh** to each word. Then circle the words in the word find below. Words go → and ↓.

1.  ____ ____ild

2. 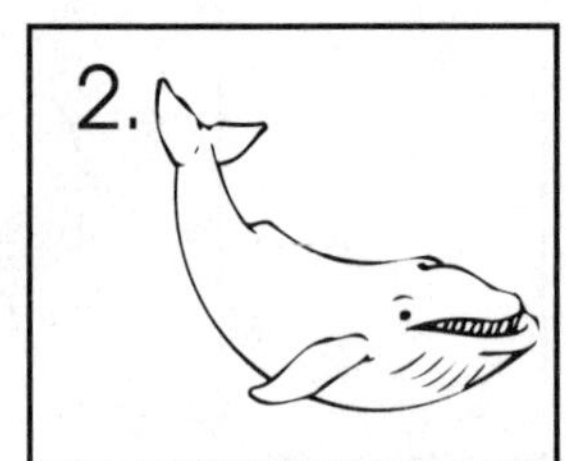 ____ ____ale

3.  cat ____ ____

4. 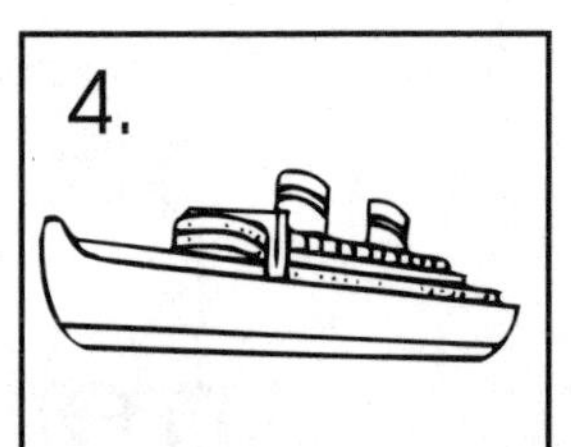 ____ ____ip

5.  wi ____ ____

6. 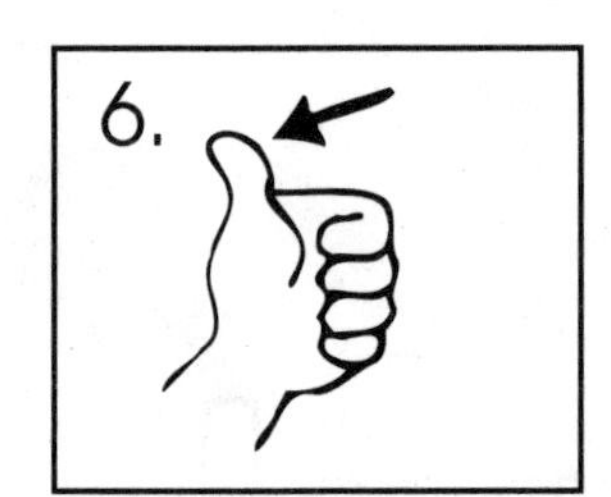 ____ ____umb

c w i s h l c
t h u m b k h
c a t c h s i
e l m f a n l
d e s h i p d

Name

Consonant blends

Unit 1

Consonant blends are two consonant letters next to each other in a word that each make their own sound.

Examples: sn in <u>sn</u>eeze, tr in <u>tr</u>ip, sl in <u>sl</u>ow

Look at the pictures. Decide what two letters are missing in each word. Write the two letters on the line.

1. 

___ ___ ee

2. 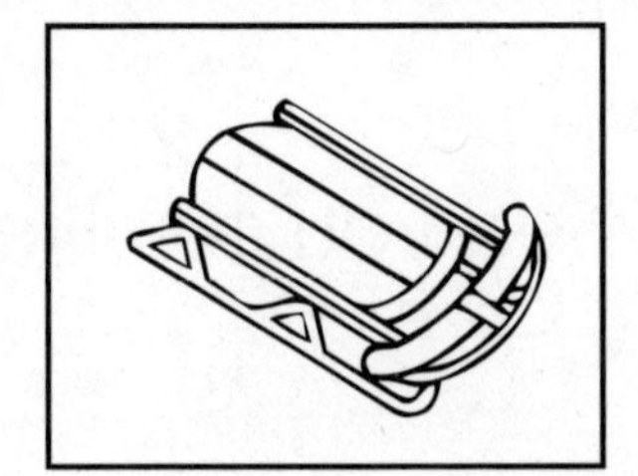

___ ___ ed

3. 

___ ___ oud

4. 

___ ___ ame

5. 

___ ___ ake

6. 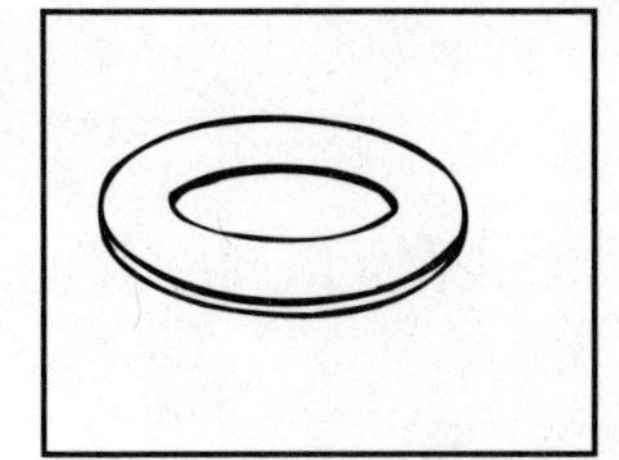

___ ___ ate

7. 

___ ___ enty

8. 

___ ___ im

9. 

___ ___ oke

10. 

___ ___ ate

11. 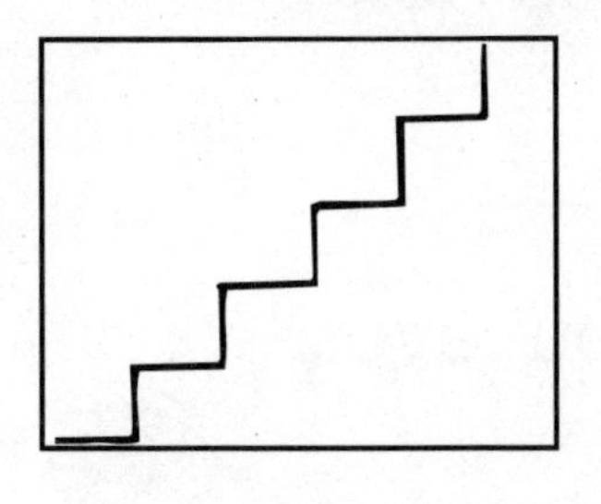

___ ___ eps

12. 

___ ___ ush

Name

Vowel digraphs

Unit 1

When two vowels are next to each other in a word they often become partners and make one sound. They are called **vowel digraphs**. The vowel digraphs ai, ea, ee, and oa often make a long vowel sound.

Examples: wait, real, see, goat

Listen to or read each clue. Look at the first letter or letters of the answer. Choose **ai**, **ea**, **ee**, or **oa** for the middle sound. Write the ending sound if needed.

1. What do you do when you are tired?

sl___ ___ ___

2. This is water that falls from the sky.

r ___ ___ ___

3. You use this in a bath.

s ___ ___ ___

4. Jack carried this up a hill.

p ___ ___ ___

5. Your ride in this on water.

b ___ ___ ___

6. You play in the sand here.

b ___ ___ ___ ___

7. You do this with your eyes.

s ___ ___

Name

y and w as vowels

Unit 1

y and **w** can sometimes make vowel sounds. Y can make the long e or long i sound like in bab<u>y</u> and cr<u>y</u>. Y and w can be silent vowel partners like in d<u>ay</u> and l<u>ow.</u>

Write the words from the Word Bank in the correct list.

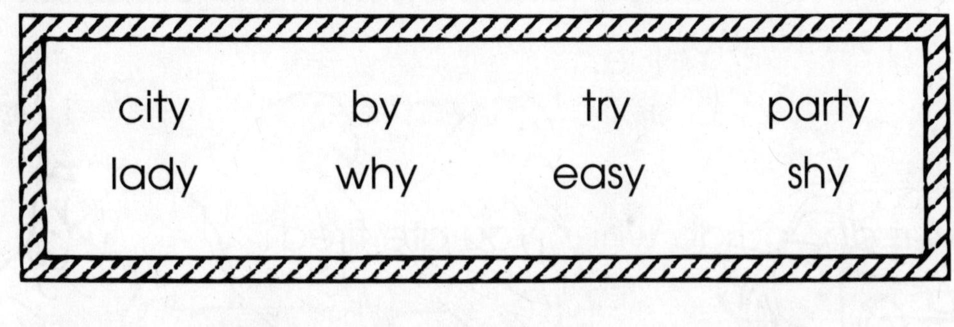

y as in baby	**y** as in cry
______________	______________
______________	______________
______________	______________
______________	______________

Look at the pictures. Add **ay** or **ow** to finish each word.

1. 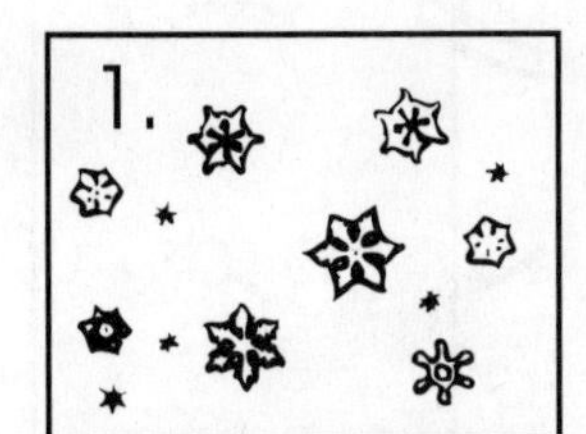

s n___ ___

2. 

h___ ___

3. 

pl___ ___

4. 

sl___ ___

5. 

bl___ ___

6. 

tr___ ___

Name

R-controlled vowels

Unit 1

When r follows most vowels, it takes control and the vowel makes a new sound.

Examples: far, her, sir, fur

Read the sentences. Write the word from the Word Bank that best finishes each sentence.

1. We ride in the ______________ to the zoo.
2. I want to be ______________ in line.
3. We see many animals with ______________.
4. The ______________ have colorful feathers.
5. We will eat ______________ the sea lion show.
6. It is ______________ when we drive home.
7. I see many ______________ in the sky.

dark
first
car
birds
stars
after
fur

Name

Unit 1 Test

Page 1

Word Analysis

Read or listen to the directions. Fill in the circle beside the best answer.

❑ Example:

Which words have the same middle sound?

Ⓐ bag, bed Ⓑ net, hit

Ⓒ log, top Ⓓ make, hat

Answer: C because the middle sound in log and top is the short o sound.

Now try these. You have 20 minutes. Continue until you see .

1. What letter makes the beginning sound of the picture?

h	l	f	n
Ⓐ	Ⓑ	Ⓒ	Ⓓ

2. Which picture has the same ending sound as **start**?

Ⓐ Ⓑ Ⓒ Ⓓ

GO ON

Name

Unit 1 Test

Page 2

3. Choose the words with different beginning sounds.

cent, circle (A) | sun, sad (B) | gift, gate (C) | city, cat (D)

4. What is the middle sound in the picture?

a (A) | e (B) | i (C) | u (D)

5. Choose the picture with the same vowel sound as in **cake**.

(A)

(B)

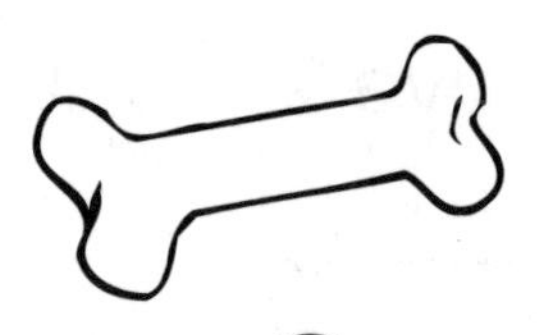
(C)

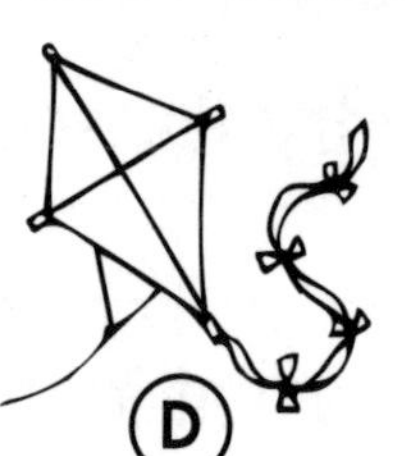
(D)

6. Which picture has the same sound as the underlined letters in the word **wi<u>sh</u>**?

(A)

(B)

(C)

(D)

7. Which word matches the picture?

cat (A) | cake (B) | car (C) | cry (D)

GO ON

Name

Unit 1 Test

8. What letters make the beginning sound in the picture?

tw (A) ck (B) dr (C) tr (D)

9. Choose the picture with the same vowel sound as in **rain**.

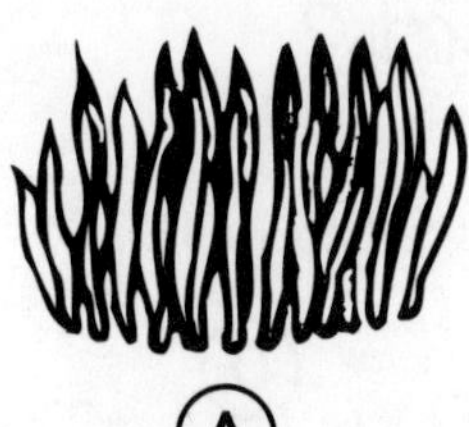

(A)

(B)

(C)

(D)

10. Which word has the same ending sound as in **lady**?

play (A) tree (B) try (C) sled (D)

11. Choose the word that best completes the sentence.

The __________ had a new dress.

girl (A) stir (B) burn (C) her (D)

12. What letter makes the ending sound in the picture?

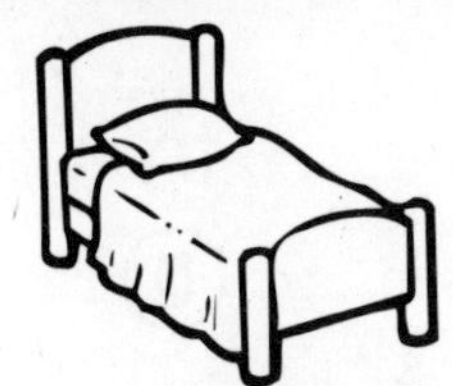

b (A) p (B) h (C) d (D)

GO ON

Name

Unit 1 Test

13. Which picture has the same beginning sound as **net**?

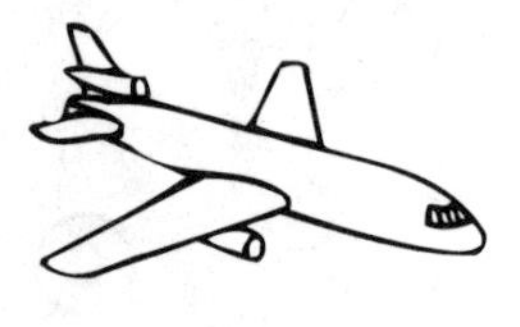

Ⓐ Ⓑ Ⓒ Ⓓ

14. The **s** makes a different sound in what two words?

sand, kiss	sun, hose	sad, swim	sit, last
Ⓐ	Ⓑ	Ⓒ	Ⓓ

15. Choose the picture with the same vowel sound as in **hop**.

Ⓐ Ⓑ Ⓒ Ⓓ

16. What word has the same middle sound as in the picture?

hit	cry	hide	dig
Ⓐ	Ⓑ	Ⓒ	Ⓓ

17. What two letters make the beginning sound in the picture?

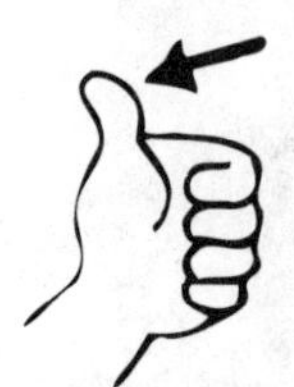

fr	ch	tr	th
Ⓐ	Ⓑ	Ⓒ	Ⓓ

GO ON

Name

Unit 1 Test

18. Which picture begins with the letters **sm**?

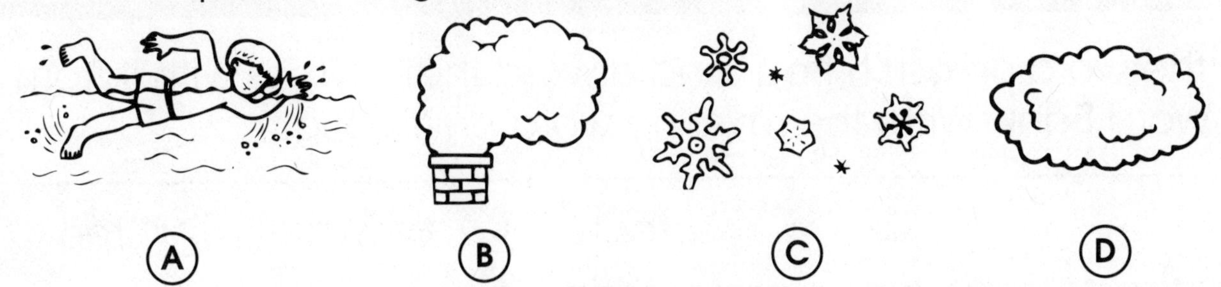

Ⓐ Ⓑ Ⓒ Ⓓ

19. Choose the word that best completes the sentence.

I saw a ________ hop in the grass.

deep	pail	boat	toad
Ⓐ	Ⓑ	Ⓒ	Ⓓ

20. What two letters finish the word sn____?

ow	ay	oo	oy
Ⓐ	Ⓑ	Ⓒ	Ⓓ

Write two words that have the same middle sound as  .

The words must have different beginning sounds.

1. ________________

2. ________________

STOP

Name

Rhyming words

Unit 2

Words that sound alike are called **rhyming words**.
The beginning sounds of the words are usually different.

Examples: cat, hat sit, hit

Say the word on each frog. Find a word that rhymes with it from the Word Bank. Write the rhyming word on the log.

boy	kiss	tent	brown	three
two	shop	day	can	

1.

2.

3.

4.

5.

6.

7.

8.

9.

Name

Compound words

Unit 2

A **compound words** is a word that is made by joining two or more words together to make a new word with a new meaning.

Example: pan + cake = pancake

Look at the picture clues. Use the words in the Word Bank to finish the compound words.

glasses	fly	tub
fish	board	mother
boy	corn	time

1. 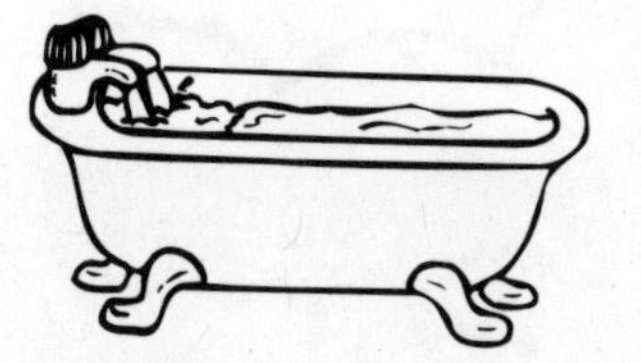

bath____________

2. 

butter____________

3. 

sun____________

4. 

pop____________

5. 

cow____________

6. 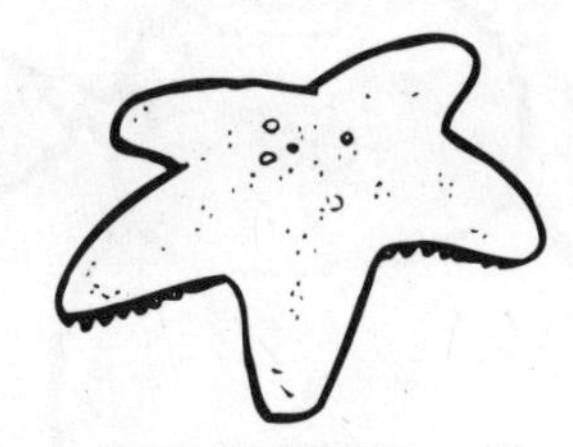

star____________

7. 

grand____________

8. 

skate____________

9. 

bed____________

Name

Synonyms

Unit 2

Synonyms are words that have the same or almost the same meaning.

Examples: small, little   big, huge

Read the word on each snowman. Choose a word in the sun that has almost the same meaning. Write it on the bottom of the snowman.

Name

Antonyms

Unit 2

Antonyms are words that have opposite meanings.

Examples: fast, slow   good, bad

Draw a line from the word bubbles on the right to the word bubbles on the left with the opposite meanings.

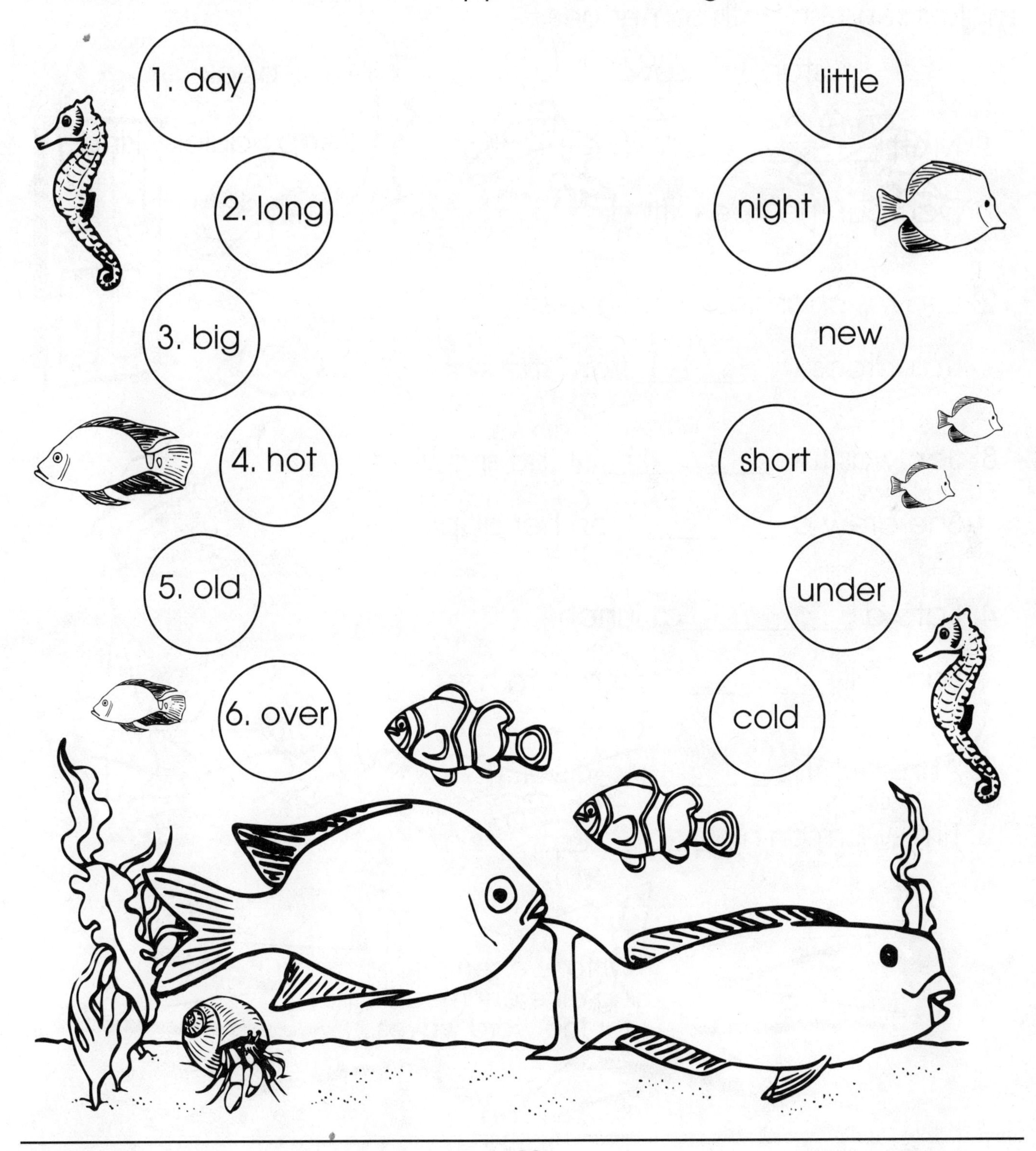

Name

Multiple meaning words

Unit 2

Some words can be spelled alike and sound alike but have different meanings. We know which meaning makes sense by reading the rest of the sentence.

Example: I turned on the fan. The fan cheered.

Read each pair of sentences. Write the word on the lines that makes sense in both sentences.

star saw fall roll back

1. Matt __________ a lion at the zoo.

   Dad cut the tree with a __________.

2. Leaves change colors in the __________.

   Raindrops __________ from the sky.

3. Jan was the __________ of the show.

   She drew a __________ on her paper.

4. I ate a __________ at lunch.

   Sam will __________ the ball to her.

5. Ann shut the __________ door.

   Tim swam on his __________.

Write two sentences using different meanings for the word **waves**.

Name

Using picture clues

Unit 2

Sometimes when you are not sure what a word is, use the picture to help you. Look at the picture and say the word for it. Next, look at the written word. Do the sounds from the picture word match the sounds in the written word?

Example:
1. Look at the picture and say the word.
2. Look at the written word.
3. Do the sounds match?

mouse

Look at the pictures. Circle the words that match the pictures.

1.  desk / dark

2.  flowers / fresh

3.  ship / shoes

4. 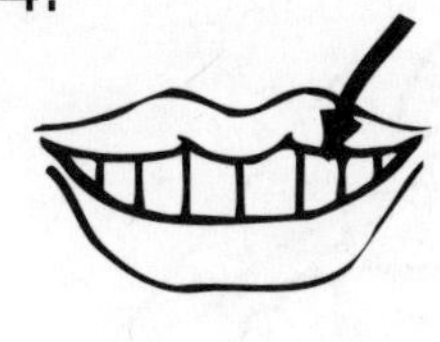 treat / teeth

5.  chick / cheese

6. 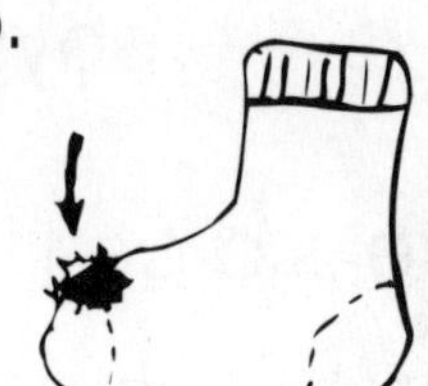 hole / hall

7.  cried / child

8.  tail / tell

9.  bake / break

10.  tree / three

11.  window / winter

12.  chair / share

Name

Using context clues

Unit 2

When you come to a word that you do not know, sometimes you can figure out the meaning from clues in the sentence.

Example: The boy giggled at the funny story. The word funny gives you a clue about the meaning of giggled. Giggled means laughed.

Use clues in the sentences to figure out the meanings of the underlined nonsense words. Circle the meanings of the words.

1. I use xapt to clean.

   fast soap time

2. The zoto hopped in the grass.

   rabbit doll car

3. We planted kibd in the garden.

   ducks boys seeds

4. There is a cefl in the sky.

   door cloud tree

5. We rode our huvot to the park.

   bikes house ball

6. You must japc your room.

   jump sleep clean

7. She went to a birthday leehm.

   party bath plant

8. The cat is niacp the basket.

   sing blow under

Name

Analyzing words through analogies

Unit 2

Analogies are one way to compare words. Look at the first set of words and decide how they are related. Now apply that same relationship to the next set of words.

Example: Dog is to bark as cat is to _____.

Dog is related to bark because bark is the sound a dog makes.
What sound does a cat make? The answer is meow.

Which dog will find the most bones? To find out, use the words on the bones to finish the analogies. Color the bones you use.

1. Red is to apple as yellow is to _______________.
2. Four is to car as two is to _______________.
3. Cold is to hot as under is to _______________.
4. Read is to book as throw is to _______________.
5. Water is to boat as snow is to _______________.
6. Fly is to bird as swim is to _______________.
7. Roof is to house as hair is to _______________.
8. Eye is to see as ear is to _______________.
9. Warm is to hot as cool is to _______________.

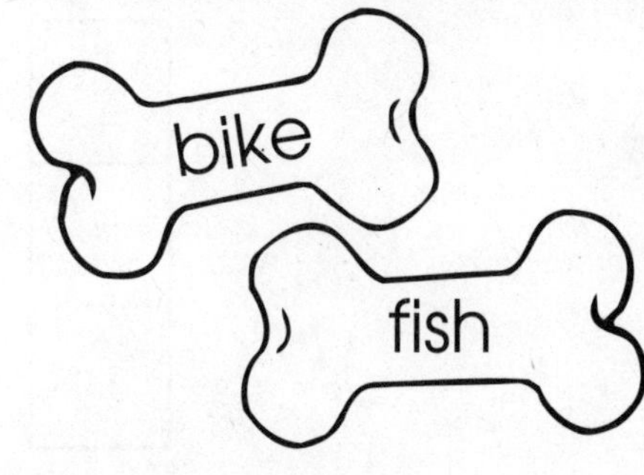

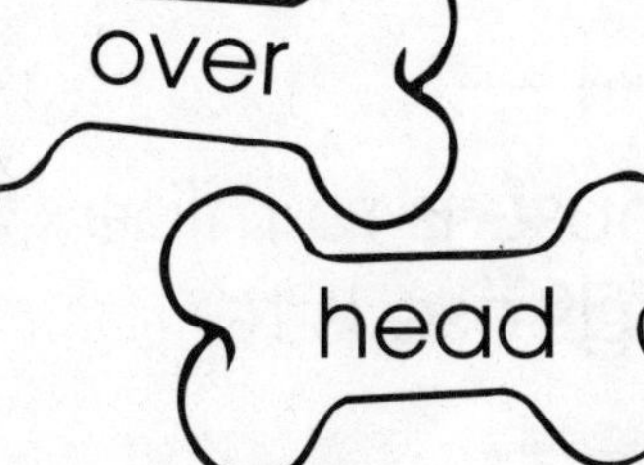

Name

Applying analogies

Unit 2

Analogies are one way to compare words. First, look for the relationship between the first set of words. Next, apply this relationship to the second set of words.

Example: Spider is to eight as horse is to ____.
Number of legs is the relationship between the first set of words.
Applying this relationship to the second set of words, the answer would be four.

Use the words in the Word Bank to solve the puzzles.

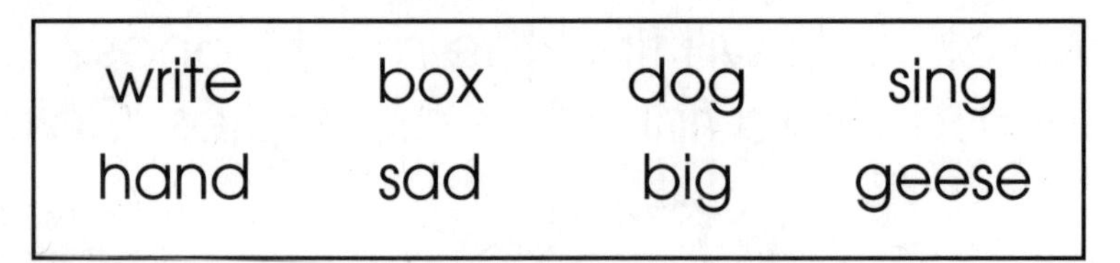

write	box	dog	sing
hand	sad	big	geese

1. Round is to ball as square is to _______.
2. Little is to small as huge is to _______.
3. Fork is to eat as pencil is to _______.
4. Cop is to mop as king is to _______.

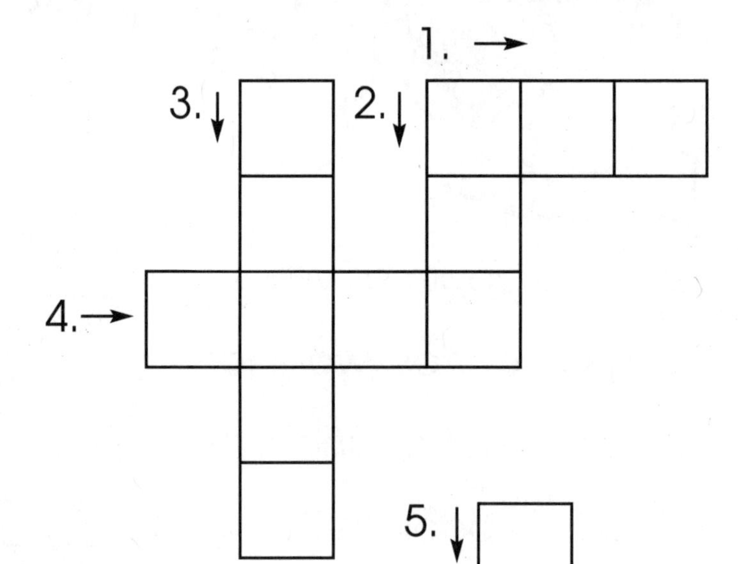

5. Hat is to head as mitten is to _______.
6. Laugh is to funny as cry is to _______.
7. Kitten is to cat as puppy is to _______.
8. Mouse is to mice as goose is to _______.

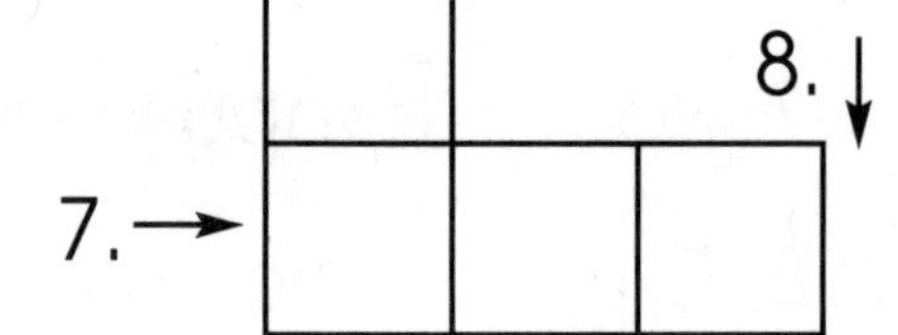

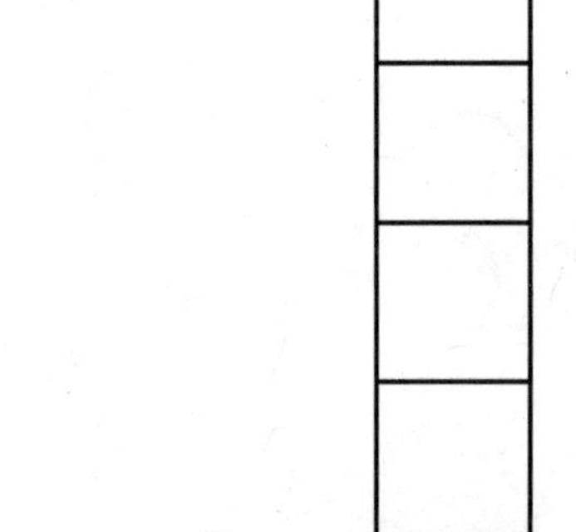

Name

Unit 2 Test

Page 1

Vocabulary Skills

Read or listen to the directions. Fill in the circle beside the best answer.

❑ Example:

Choose the word with the same meaning as **tiny**.

Ⓐ big Ⓑ shiny

Ⓒ time Ⓓ small

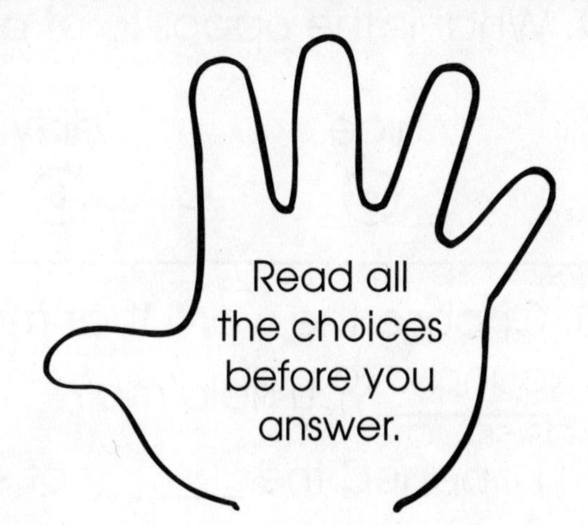

Answer: D because tiny and small have the same meaning.

Now try these. You have 20 minutes. Continue until you see STOP.

1. What word rhymes with  ?

step	car	stare	shore
Ⓐ	Ⓑ	Ⓒ	Ⓓ

2. Which word is not a compound word?

Ⓐ skateboard Ⓑ bedtime

Ⓒ children Ⓓ classroom

3. Choose the word with the same meaning as **finish**.

end	begin	wish	find
Ⓐ	Ⓑ	Ⓒ	Ⓓ

GO ON

Name

Unit 2 Test

Page 2

4. What is the opposite of **clean**?

nice	dirty	mean	clear
(A)	(B)	(C)	(D)

5. Choose the word that makes sense in both sentences.

_______ you help me?

I opened the _______ of soup.

cup	will	eat	can
(A)	(B)	(C)	(D)

6. Which word matches the picture?

cloud	clown	could	cold
(A)	(B)	(C)	(D)

7. Choose the word to finish the sentence.

I wear a _______ when it is cold.

snow	shorts	coat	winter
(A)	(B)	(C)	(D)

GO ON

Name

Unit 2 Test

8. Fire is to hot as ice is to ______.

warm	water	cold	mice
(A)	(B)	(C)	(D)

9. Which word does not rhyme with  ?

how	now	wow	low
(A)	(B)	(C)	(D)

10. Which picture names a compound word?

(A)	(B)	(C)	(D)

11. Choose the word with the same meaning as **beside**.

by	over	hide	out
(A)	(B)	(C)	(D)

12. What is the opposite of **tall**?

big	short	hall	man
(A)	(B)	(C)	(D)

GO ON

Name

Unit 2 Test

Page 4

13. Choose the word that makes sense in both sentences.

She _______ her hand when I go.

There are _______ in the ocean.

shakes	water	waves	wait
(A)	(B)	(C)	(D)

14. Read the sentence. Mark the picture that matches the underlined word.

We climbed the mountain.

(A) (B) (C) (D)

15. Choose the word to finish the sentence.

He went to _______ because he was tired.

sleep	play	eat	fish
(A)	(B)	(C)	(D)

16. Wow! Jan drew a terrific picture.

Terrific means _______.

silly	great	not good	small
(A)	(B)	(C)	(D)

GO ON

Name

Unit 2 Test

17. Box is to fox as make is to ________.

socks (A) map (B) lake (C) date (D)

18. Mark the word that makes sense in the sentence.

I read the ________ to my sister.

game (A) book (B) toy (C) box (D)

19. Choose the word that makes sense in both sentences.

The window is ________.

________ your desk.

glass (A) move (B) inside (C) clear (D)

20. Right is to left as up is to ________.

over (A) down (B) cup (C) sky (D)

Think of a word that means the same as **big**. Write a sentence using that word.

____

STOP

Name

Following directions **Unit 3**

Directions are steps for doing something. Always be sure to do each step in order. Do not skip any steps. Pay attention to key words such as number words and color words.

Help Tanner and Andy finish building their clubhouse. Follow each step in order.

1. Draw two square windows.
2. Write **Clubhouse** above the door.
3. Draw a rectangle around the word **Clubhouse**.
4. Color the clubhouse brown.
5. Color the door red.
6. Draw a roof. Color it green.
7. Draw yourself near the clubhouse.

Name

Following directions **Unit 3**

Directions are steps for doing something. Be sure to read all the directions carefully. Pay close attention to the key words such as above, inside, and underneath.

Follow the directions.

1. Write the word **book**. Draw a square above the word.	2. Draw a rectangle. Draw two triangles inside of the rectangle.
3. Write the word **plane**. Draw a line underneath the word.	4. Draw a circle. Draw a line through the circle.
5. Draw a square. Draw a small square above it. Write the word **dog** inside the larger square.	6. Write the word **car**. Draw two circles below the word. Draw a triangle above the word.

Name

Classifying groups

Unit 3

Things can be grouped together because they are alike in some way.

Example:  These could be classified as a group of bugs.

Decide what the things in each picture have in common. Choose a group name from the Word Bank for each picture. Write it on the line.

pets	shapes	things that go
things to eat	farm animals	tools

1. 

2. 

3. 

4. 

5. 

6. 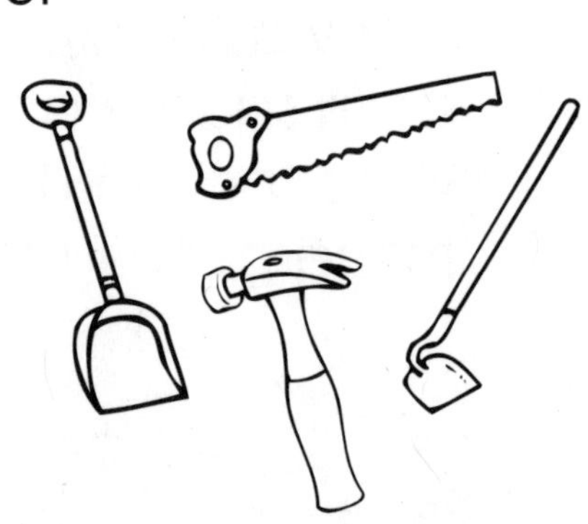

Name

Classifying words

Unit 3

Words that are alike in some way can be classified, or grouped, together.

Example: red, green, blue These words can be grouped together as color words.

Read the words in each row. Cross out the word that does not belong with the other words.

Example:	plate	~~door~~	spoon	cup
1.	jump	skip	run	dog
2.	car	arms	legs	hands
3.	roof	window	toys	door
4.	den	girl	hive	cave
5.	pencil	crayon	marker	paper
6.	sit	sing	talk	yell

Name another word for each word group above. Think of a group name for each group of words.

Name

Alphabetical order—letters

Unit 3

To put a group of letters in alphabetical order, follow these steps:

1. Look at all the letters
2. Decide which letter comes first. Write it down.
3. Decide which letter comes next. Write it down.
4. Continue until you have used all the letters.

Example: i b f → b → b f → b f i

Use the alphabet chart to help write the groups of letters in alphabetical order. Then write the circled letters in order on the blanks below to solve the riddle.

A	B	C	D	E	F	G	H	I	J	K	L	M	N	O	P	Q	R	S	T	U	V	W	X	Y	Z
a	b	c	d	e	f	g	h	i	j	k	l	m	n	o	p	q	r	s	t	u	v	w	x	y	z

1. V T Y
◯ ___ ___

2. o j h
◯ ___ ___

3. h e d
___ ◯ ___

4. s m p
___ ___ ◯

5. f c i
___ ___ ◯

6. n q g
___ ◯ ___

7. t w s
◯ ___ ___

8. h b n
___ ◯ ___

9. y o u
◯ ___ ___

10. i l h
___ ___ ◯

Why are fish so smart?

_ _ _ y   _ w _ m   i _   _ c _ _ o _ s.

Name

Alphabetical order—words

Unit 3

Many groups of words are listed in alphabetical order.
To put a group of words in alphabetical order follow these steps:

	1. Look at the first letter of each word.	2. Decide which letter comes first.	3. Write down this word.	4. Continue until you have used all the words.
Example:	cat, bat, fat	b	bat	bat, cat, fat

Write the words on the cones in alphabetical order.

1.

1. ____________
2. ____________
3. ____________

man
can
tan

2.

1. ____________
2. ____________
3. ____________

tree
grass
sky

3.

1. ____________
2. ____________
3. ____________

four
nine
one

4.

1. ____________
2. ____________
3. ____________

pink
blue
red

5.

1. ____________
2. ____________
3. ____________

crab
shell
frog

6.

1. ____________
2. ____________
3. ____________

wolf
lion
fox

Name

Using a title page

Unit 3

The first page of a book is usually the title page. It tells the title of the book, who wrote the book (the author), and who made the pictures (the illustrator).

title → **The Magic Sled**

by
Jane Brown ← author

Illustrated by
illustrator → Kyle Moore

Find two books. Write the title, author, and illustrator of each book on the title pages below.

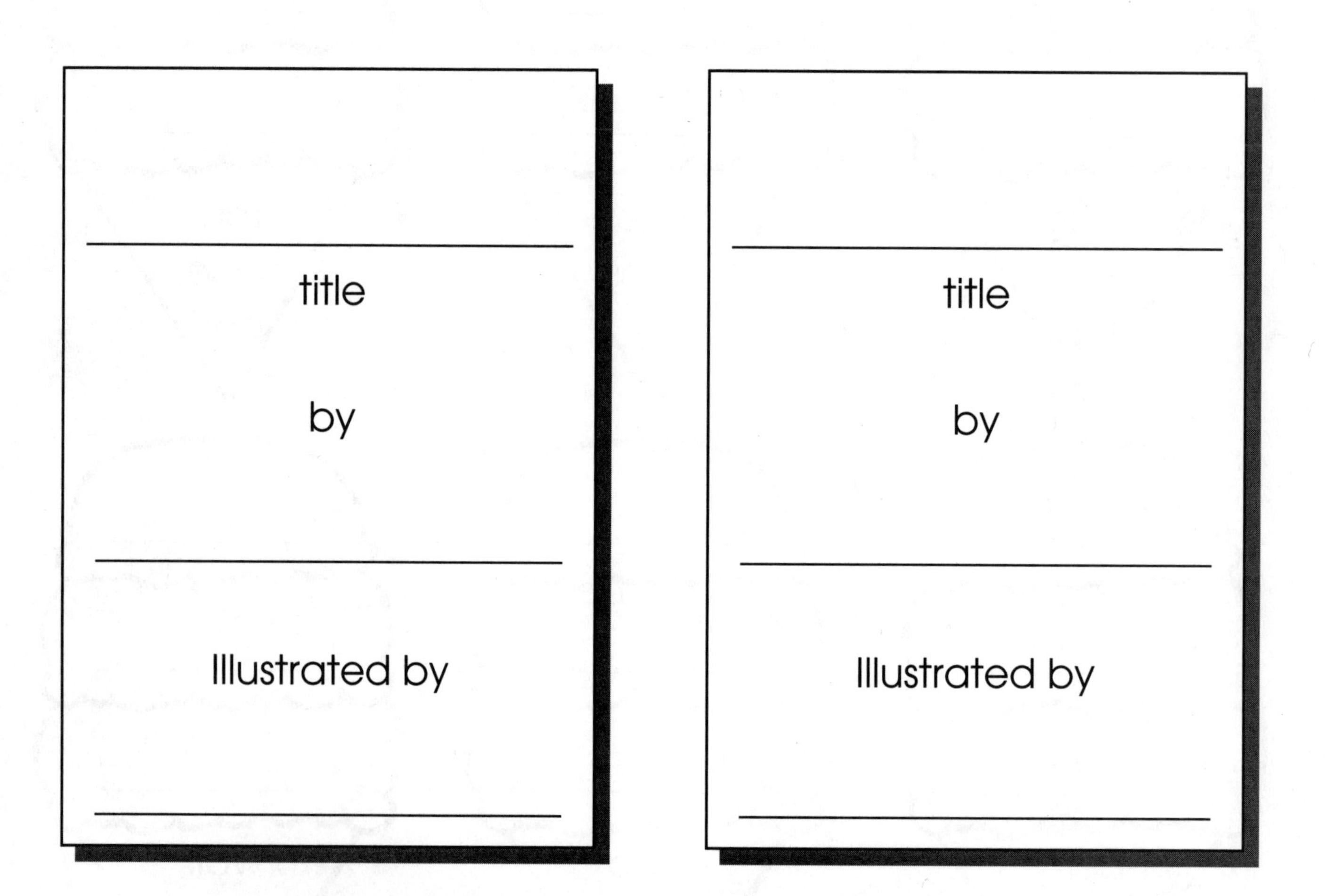

Name

Using a table of contents

Unit 3

Most chapter books and longer informational books have a table of contents after the title page. The table of contents tells the beginning page number for the chapters or topics in the book.

Use the table of contents to answer the questions.

Table of Contents

1. The title of Chapter 2 is ______________________________.
2. Chapter _______ begins on page 15.
3. How many chapters are in the book? _______
4. Chapter _______ would tell you about brown bats.
5. Bats have a thumb on their wings. Chapter _______ would tell you this fact.
6. Chapter _______ will tell you what bats eat.
7. Chapter 4 begins on page _______.

Name

Unit 3 Test

Page 1

Study Skills

Read or listen to the directions. Fill in the circle beside the best answer.

❑ Example:

Which word does not belong?

Ⓐ white Ⓑ black

Ⓒ blue Ⓓ nine

Answer: D because it is not a color word.

Now try these. You have 20 minutes. Continue until you see STOP.

1. Draw a circle.
   Draw a small circle inside the circle.
   Draw an X below the circles.

   Mark the picture that shows the directions followed correctly.

   X X X X

   Ⓐ Ⓑ Ⓒ Ⓓ

2. What is the best group name for the pictures?

Ⓐ things that are red Ⓑ things to eat

Ⓒ things with wheels Ⓓ things that are small

Name

Unit 3 Test

3. Which word does not belong with the other words?

car (A) truck (B) school (C) van (D)

4. Which letters are in alphabetical order?

b a c (A) d e f (B) j i h (C) r t s (D)

5. Choose the word that comes first in alphabetical order.

dog (A) cat (B) bug (C) fox (D)

6. Write the word **stop**.
Draw a square above the word.
Draw a line underneath the word.
Mark the picture that shows the directions followed correctly.

stop (A) stop (B) stop (C) stop (D)

GO ON

Name

Unit 3 Test

Page 3

Use the title page to answer questions 7–9.

The Hot Day

by
Matt Woods

Illustrated by
Ann Last

7. The title of the book is ___________.

(A) Matt Woods
(B) Ann Last
(C) The Hot Day
(D) Illustrated by

8. What did Ann Last do?

(A) wrote the book
(B) drew the pictures
(C) sold the book
(D) read the book

9. The author is ___________.

(A) Matt Woods
(B) Ann Last
(C) Illustrated
(D) The Hot Day

10. Which word does not belong in the group?

water	milk	soda	cheese
(A)	(B)	(C)	(D)

11. Which letters are in alphabetical order?

Y Q X	M P T	K G N	F B D
(A)	(B)	(C)	(D)

GO ON

Name

Unit 3 Test

Use the Table of Contents to answer questions 12–14.

12. Chapter _____ begins on page 9.

1	2	3	4
Ⓐ	Ⓑ	Ⓒ	Ⓓ

13. How many chapters are in the book?

4	6	9	12
Ⓐ	Ⓑ	Ⓒ	Ⓓ

14. Read Chapter _____ to find out about cats.

1	2	3	4
Ⓐ	Ⓑ	Ⓒ	Ⓓ

15. Which word does not belong?

five	ten	six	blue
Ⓐ	Ⓑ	Ⓒ	Ⓓ

GO ON

Name

16. Which picture shows the directions followed correctly?

Draw a tall tree on the left.

Draw a short tree on the right.

Draw a flower in the middle.

Ⓐ

Ⓑ

Ⓒ

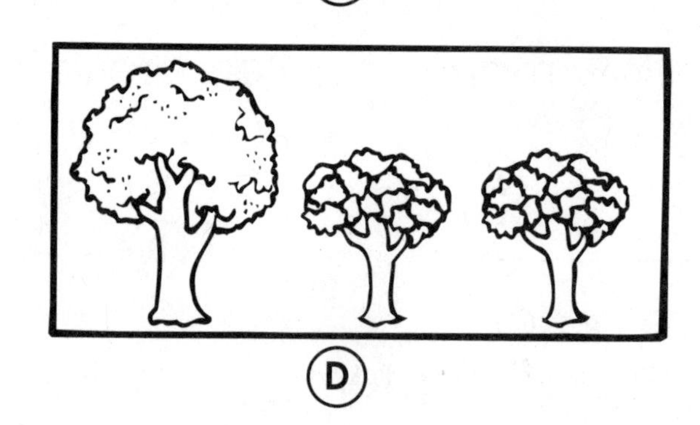

Ⓓ

17. Choose the best group name.

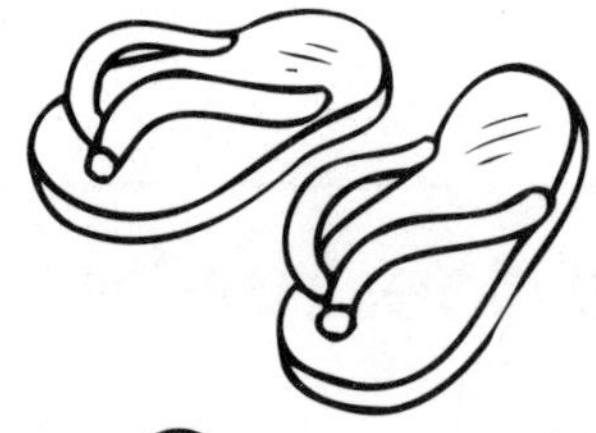

Ⓐ clothes

Ⓑ shoes

Ⓒ sports

Ⓓ walk

GO ON

Name

Unit 3 Test

18. Which word is like these words?

cloud moon sun

star (A) land (B) tree (C) shine (D)

19. Which letters are not in alphabetical order?

b d f (A) a m k (B) n p r (C) u x z (D)

20. Which word comes last in alphabetical order?

box (A) egg (B) go (C) man (D)

Write directions for the picture.

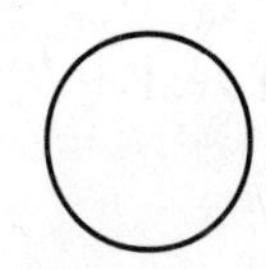

X

STOP

Name

A picture title

Unit 4

The title of a picture or a story tells what it is mostly about.

Circle the best title for each picture.

1\.

Fish in the Sea

My Pet Fish

2\.

A Trip to the Moon

Planet Earth

3\.

A Day at the Beach

Fun at the Pool

4\.

A Bird Adventure

The Plane Ride

5\.

I'm All Wet!

The Rain Cloud

6\.

The Cat and Dog

The Cat Picture

Write your own title for the picture.

7\.

____

Draw a picture. Write a title for your picture.

Name

A story title Unit 4

A story is always about something. The sentences tell you what the story is about. The title helps tell you what the story is mostly about.

The titles at the bottom tell what each story is mostly about. Cut each one out and glue it at the top of the story it matches.

1. Sally made a wish every night before going to sleep. She would look in the sky for the brightest star. Then she would close her eyes and make a wish.	2. Sally fell asleep in the car on the way to the zoo. She dreamed that she was a flying turtle. She flew all around the zoo. No one could catch her.
3. Sally had her friend Jill sleep over. They watched a video and ate popcorn. They made a tent out of blankets. They slept in the tent.	4. Sally woke up very early. She was very excited. Today her family was getting a new puppy. They had already named the puppy Muffet.

The Turtle Dream	**The Sleepover**
A New Puppy	**A Wish Before Bed**

Name

Main idea

Unit 4

The main idea of a story is what the story is mostly about.

Read the stories. Fill in the circles that tell the main ideas.

1. George Washington grew up in Virginia. He liked to play games outside. He also helped his family on their farm. When he was seven, he started school.

Ⓐ George Washington was the first president.

Ⓑ George Washington grew up in Virginia.

Ⓒ George Washington went to school.

2. Abe Lincoln had many different jobs. He worked as a farmer and a carpenter. He also helped on riverboats. Abe worked at a store. Later, he became a lawyer.

Ⓐ Abe Lincoln was born in a log cabin.

Ⓑ Abe Lincoln liked to read books.

Ⓒ Abe Lincoln had many different jobs.

3. Martin Luther King, Jr., won the Nobel Peace Prize. This prize is given to a person who has worked hard for peace. The prize is money. He gave the money to people who helped him work for peace.

Ⓐ Martin Luther King, Jr., won the Nobel Peace Prize.

Ⓑ Martin Luther King, Jr., believed all people were born equal.

Ⓒ We celebrate Martin Luther King, Jr., Day in January.

Name

Story facts Unit 4

Story facts (or details) help you understand what the story is about.
Story facts help you answer questions about the story.

Tara's Birthday

Tara celebrated her seventh birthday on Saturday. She had a very busy day.

In the morning she went to breakfast with her grandma. She ordered a big plate of pancakes. She ate every one.

In the afternoon Tara and six friends went to a movie. After the movie they went for ice cream cones. Then they all went back to Tara's house to open her presents.

For dinner Tara's mom fixed Tara her favorite meal. She fixed grilled cheese sandwiches and watermelon. She also baked a chocolate cake with white icing. It was delicious!

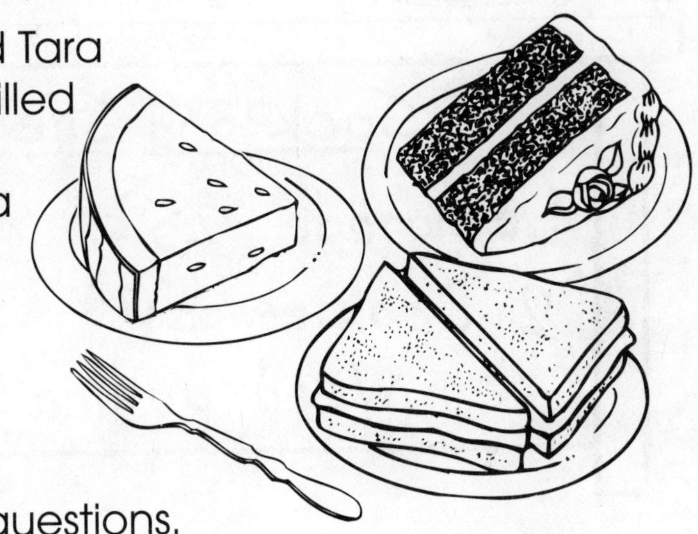

Tara was very tired when she went to bed.

Use story facts to answer the questions.

1. How old is Tara now? ______________________
2. What did she eat for breakfast? ______________________
3. Where did Tara open her presents? ______________________
4. What is Tara's favorite meal? ______________________

____

5. What kind of cake did Tara's mom bake? ______________________

____

Name

Using facts

Unit 4

Facts tell you important information.

Use the facts from the sign to answer the questions.

1. Who works at the store? ______________________
2. How much is lemonade? ______________________
3. How many cookies do you get for 50 cents? __________
4. How far does a dog get walked? ______________________

   ____
5. What job costs $1 per hour? ______________________

Name

Finding facts Unit 4

Facts are important information about a subject. You can use the facts to answer questions about the subject. You may need to look back in the story to find the facts you need.

A Bullfrog's Habitat

Habitat is another name for an animal home. A creek near some woods is a good habitat for a bullfrog. There are lots of insects for the frogs to eat. There are also places for them to hide. The quiet water is a good place for them to lay their eggs. This habitat gives bullfrogs everything they need to live.

Use the facts to answer the questions.

1. Another name for an animal home is a ______________________.
2. What is a good habitat for a bullfrog? ______________________

   ____
3. Bullfrogs eat ________________________________.
4. Bullfrogs lay their eggs in __________________ water.
5. This habitat gives bullfrogs everything they __________________

   ____.

Name

Reality and fantasy

Unit 4

Some stories are about things that can really happen. These are reality stories.
Some stories are about things that could not really happen. These are fantasy stories.

Example: The mouse ran under the chair. (Reality)
The mouse rode a bike. (Fantasy)

Color the turtles that tell about something that could really happen.

Name

Real or fantasy

Unit 4

The events in a story can be divided into two groups: real (events that can really happen) and fantasy (events that are make-believe).

The clouds below tell a story. Read them in order. Color the clouds that are fantasy blue and the clouds that are real yellow. The blue clouds will make a path for the mouse to follow.

1. Once upon a time there was a mouse that was a king. His name was King Moe.
2. The mouse lived in an old barn.
3. Cows, pigs, and chickens lived in the barn.
4. King Moe wore a crown and a purple robe wherever he went.
5. He ordered the cows and pigs to plant corn. They worked very hard.
6. The chickens had to sing to King Moe morning, noon, and night.
7. Kelly lived in the house by the barn.
8. King Moe liked to talk to Kelly. Kelly and the king were friends.
9. Kelly told King Moe that he should not make the other animals work so hard.
10. The other animals were very tired.
11. So, King Moe took the animals to the beach for a vacation.

Name

Unit 4 Test

Page 1

Main Idea, Recognizing Facts, Reality and Fantasy

Read or listen to the directions. Fill in the circle beside the best answer.

❑ Example:

What could not really happen?

- Ⓐ Sam rode his scooter to the park.
- Ⓑ His dog, Bud, rode a bike.
- Ⓒ Sam threw the ball to Bud.
- Ⓓ Bud brought the ball back to Sam.

Answer: B because a dog could not ride a bike to the park.

Now try these. You have 25 minutes. Continue until you see .

1. Choose the best title for the picture.

- Ⓐ The Kite in the Tree
- Ⓑ Making a Kite
- Ⓒ The Red and Yellow Kite
- Ⓓ Flying My Kite

2. Choose the title of a story that could not really happen.

- Ⓐ The Fastest Horse
- Ⓑ My Golden Horse
- Ⓒ The Jumping Horse
- Ⓓ My Talking Horse

Name

Unit 4 Test

Read the story to answer questions 3–5.

Mother Dog was cooking dinner. It was six o'clock. Five puppies were playing with two balls. Father Dog was asleep. Mother Dog told the puppies to wake up Father Dog. The puppies started barking. Father Dog woke up. The puppies were excited to see Father Dog. They licked his face.

3. How many puppies are in the story?

two	three	five	six
Ⓐ	Ⓑ	Ⓒ	Ⓓ

4. What could not really happen?

Ⓐ Mother Dog was cooking dinner.
Ⓑ Five puppies were playing with two balls.
Ⓒ Father Dog was asleep.
Ⓓ The puppies started barking.

5. Why did Father Dog wake up?

Ⓐ He smelled dinner.
Ⓑ He heard the puppies playing.
Ⓒ The puppies licked his face.
Ⓓ The puppies started barking.

Name

Unit 4 Test

Read the story to answer questions 6 and 7.

The first American flag had 13 red and white stripes. It also had 13 white stars on a blue square. Many people think Betsy Ross sewed the first flag. They also think General George Washington asked her to do this.

6. What is the best title for this story?

Ⓐ Betsy Ross
Ⓑ The First American Flag
Ⓒ Thirteen Stars
Ⓓ General George Washington

7. What colors were the stars on the flag?

blue	red	yellow	white
Ⓐ	Ⓑ	Ⓒ	Ⓓ

8. Mark the best title for the picture.

Ⓐ The Hopping Frog
Ⓑ The Smart Frog
Ⓒ The Frog Goes Swimming
Ⓓ The Happy Frog

GO ON

Name

Unit 4 Test

Page 4

Use the sign to answer questions 9–11.

Hot Dog	50¢	Chips	25¢
Hamburger	75¢	Soda	50¢
Pizza Slice	50¢	Juice	75¢
3 Tacos	75¢	Popcorn	50¢
French Fries	50¢	Cookie	25¢

9. Choose the best title for the sign.

Ⓐ A Hot Dog Stand
Ⓑ Fries and Chips
Ⓒ Tasty Foods
Ⓓ Ice Cold Drinks

10. How many items cost 75 cents?

one Ⓐ
two Ⓑ
three Ⓒ
four Ⓓ

11. What foods cost 25 cents?

Ⓐ cookie and chips
Ⓑ 3 tacos and chips
Ⓒ juice and popcorn
Ⓓ cookie and 3 tacos

GO ON

Name

Unit 4 Test

Read the story to answer questions 12–14.

Chinese New Year is a very important holiday. It has been celebrated for thousands of years. This holiday lasts for 15 days. There is a parade at the end of the holiday. It is called the dragon parade.

12. What is the main idea of the story?

Ⓐ Families have feasts.
Ⓑ There is a dragon parade.
Ⓒ Chinese New Year is an important holiday.
Ⓓ Chinese New Year began thousands of years ago.

13. How long does Chinese New Year last?

Ⓐ thousands of years
Ⓑ 15 days
Ⓒ one day
Ⓓ a week

14. What happens at the end of Chinese New Year?

Ⓐ a parade
Ⓑ a feast
Ⓒ a game
Ⓓ a dance

GO ON

Name

Unit 4 Test

Page 6

Read the story to answer questions 15 and 16.

One kind of whale is the humpback whale. These whales make very strange sounds. It sounds like they are singing. Their songs can be beautiful. Humpback whales are funny looking. Bumps cover their heads. Like all other whales, they are not fish. They are mammals.

15. What is the main idea?

Ⓐ Humpback whales are one kind of whale.
Ⓑ Humpback whales make strange sounds.
Ⓒ Humpback whales have bumps on their heads.
Ⓓ Humpback whales are not fish.

16. What is not a fact from the story?

Ⓐ Humpback whales have bumps on their heads.
Ⓑ Whales are not fish.
Ⓒ All whales are the same size.
Ⓓ Humpback whales make strange sounds.

17. Choose the best title for the pictures.

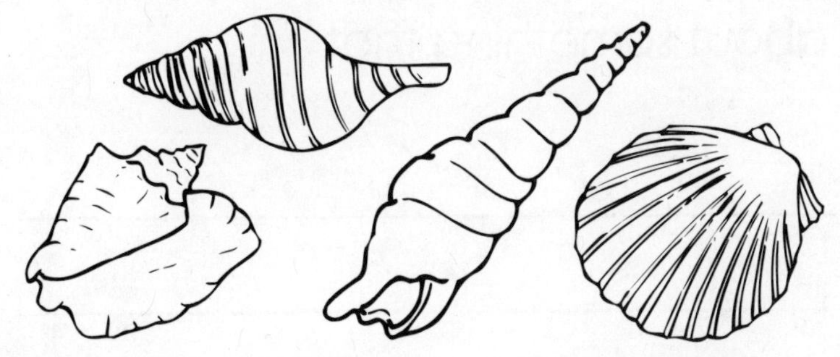

Ⓐ At the Beach
Ⓑ The Ocean
Ⓒ Small Seashells
Ⓓ Many Seashells

Name

Unit 4 Test

18. What could not happen?

Ⓐ The teacher rode her bike to school.
Ⓑ She skipped along the sidewalk.
Ⓒ At recess she went down the slide.
Ⓓ She gave each duck a pencil.

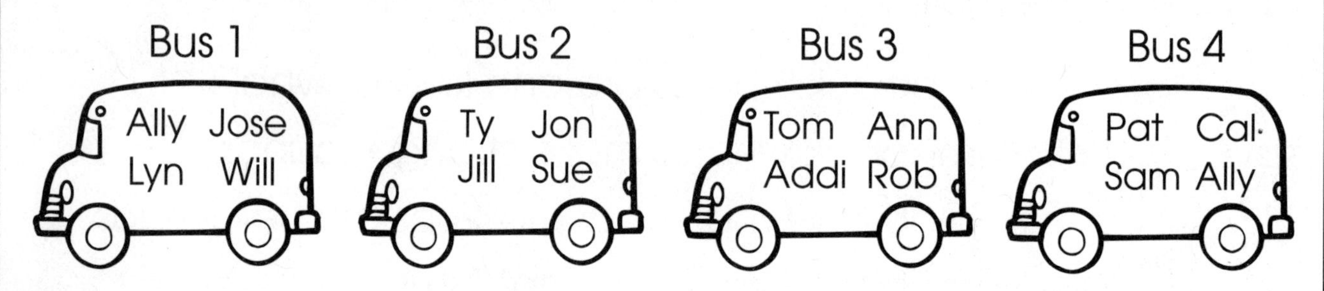

19. Which bus does Jon ride?

1	2	3	4
Ⓐ	Ⓑ	Ⓒ	Ⓓ

20. There are children named Ally on which buses?

Ⓐ Bus 1 and Bus 2
Ⓑ Bus 2 and Bus 4
Ⓒ Bus 1 and Bus 4
Ⓓ Bus 1 and Bus 3

Write a sentence that tells about something that could not happen.

____

____

STOP

Name

Midway Review Test

Page 1

Read or listen to the directions. Fill in the circle beside the best answer.

❑ Example:

Cone rhymes with _____.

Ⓐ gone

Ⓑ home

Ⓒ tone

Ⓓ soon

Answer: C because **cone** and **tone** rhyme.

Now try these. You have 25 minutes.

Continue until you see STOP.

Remember your Helping Hand Strategies:

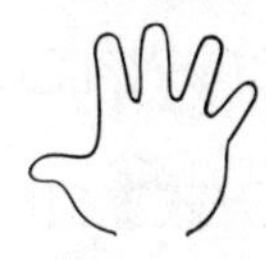

1. Whisper the sounds you are making to yourself.

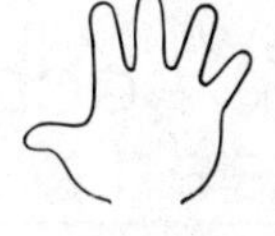

2. Read all the choices before you answer.

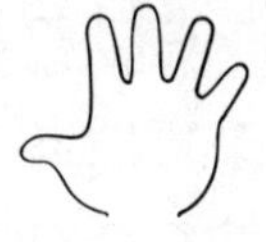

3. If you are unsure, try each answer in the blank.

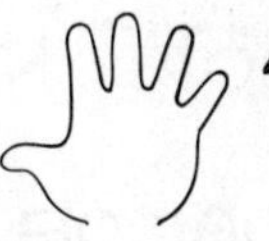

4. Read carefully and go back to the story if you are unsure.

1. What is the ending sound in 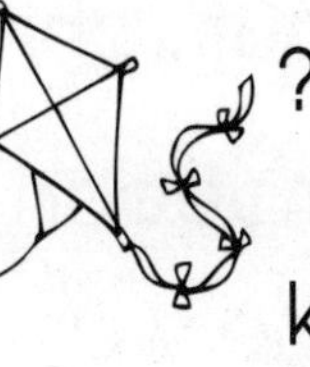 ?

e	t	k	i
Ⓐ	Ⓑ	Ⓒ	Ⓓ

2. Choose the word with same meaning as **night**.

light	day	evening	nine
Ⓐ	Ⓑ	Ⓒ	Ⓓ

GO ON

Name

Midway Review Test

Page 2

3. Which letters are not in alphabetical order?

h e k	a f i	m p r	w x z
Ⓐ	Ⓑ	Ⓒ	Ⓓ

Read the story to answer questions 4 and 5.

Johnny Appleseed planted apple seeds for 49 years. He lived over 200 years ago. His real name was John Chapman. He walked barefoot around the country planting apple orchards. Some of the apple trees he planted still make apples.

4. Choose the title that tells what the story is mostly about.

Ⓐ Making Apple Pie
Ⓑ Walking Barefoot
Ⓒ Johnny Appleseed
Ⓓ Eating an Apple

5. What is not a fact about Johnny Appleseed?

Ⓐ He planted peach seeds.
Ⓑ His real name was John Chapman.
Ⓒ He planted apple seeds for 49 years.
Ⓓ He lived over 200 years ago.

6. Mark the word with the same middle sound as .

ten	top	cut	dig
Ⓐ	Ⓑ	Ⓒ	Ⓓ

GO ON

Name

Midway Review Test

7. Square is to box as circle is to ______.

shape	egg	ball	zero
(A)	(B)	(C)	(D)

8. Which word does not belong?

(A) banana (B) bowl
(C) apple (D) strawberry

9. What word makes the same beginning sound as  ?

tree	free	chin	think
(A)	(B)	(C)	(D)

10. The spider made a ______ .

web	leg	ball	zero
(A)	(B)	(C)	(D)

11. Mark the compound word.

(A) jackets (B) sunshine
(C) basement (D) camping

GO ON

Name

Midway Review Test

Use the title page and table of contents to answer questions 12–14.

My Pets by Ann White Illustrated by Scott Allen	Chapter 1 Our Dog Ginger .....3 Chapter 2 The Hermit Crab ....6 Chapter 3 The Three Kittens ...8 Chapter 4 Fluffy the Bunny ...11

12. Who wrote the book?

Ⓐ Ann White Ⓑ Ginger

Ⓒ Scott Allen Ⓓ My Pets

13. On what page does Chapter 2 begin?

3	6	8	11
Ⓐ	Ⓑ	Ⓒ	Ⓓ

14. What is the title of Chapter 1?

Ⓐ The Three Kittens Ⓑ The Hermit Crab

Ⓒ Our Dog Ginger Ⓓ Fluffy the Bunny

GO ON

Name

Midway Review Test

Read the story to answer questions 15–17.

Rain was falling outside. Thunder roared. Lightning lit the sky. Inside, Liz was looking for her kitten, Mandy. Mandy was afraid of storms. Mandy hid when she was scared. Liz looked all over the house. Liz was sad she could not find Mandy. Liz went to her room. She heard something crying. Mandy was hiding under Liz's bed. Liz was happy.

15. Choose the best title for the story.

Ⓐ It's Raining
Ⓑ The Thunder Is Loud
Ⓒ Liz Is Happy
Ⓓ Where Is Mandy?

16. Where was Mandy hiding?

Ⓐ under Liz's bed
Ⓑ under a chair
Ⓒ outside
Ⓓ in the basement

17. Who is looking for the kitten?

Ⓐ Mandy
Ⓑ Liz
Ⓒ the mother
Ⓓ a cat

GO ON

Name

Midway Review Test

Page 6

18. City has the same ending sound as _____.

eat	candy	circle	kiss
Ⓐ	Ⓑ	Ⓒ	Ⓓ

19. He won _____ place in the race.

fern	far	fur	first
Ⓐ	Ⓑ	Ⓒ	Ⓓ

20. The opposite of **fast** is _____.

quick	last	slow	fit
Ⓐ	Ⓑ	Ⓒ	Ⓓ

Write directions for the picture.

X

___

____

____

____

STOP

Name

Sequencing pictures

Unit 5

Sequencing means putting events from a story in the order they happened.
A picture story can be put in order by looking at details in the pictures.

Example: Use the details to help you decide which picture would happen <u>first</u>. Next, decide which picture would happen <u>second</u>. Last, decide which picture would happen <u>third</u>.

Number the pictures **1**, **2**, or **3** in the order they would happen.

1.

____

____

____

2.

____

____

____

3.

____

____

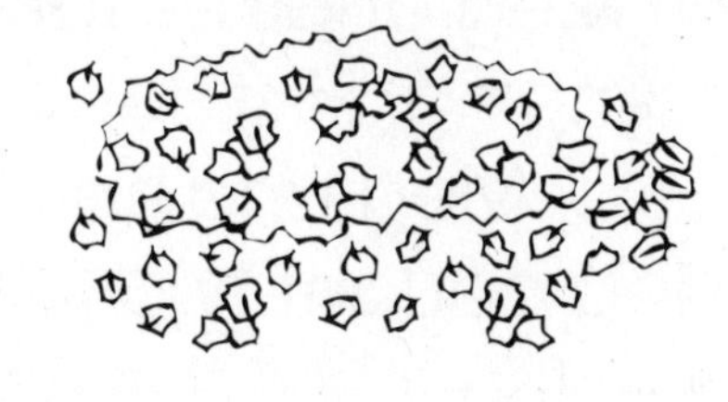

____

4.

____

____

____

Name

Sequence of a story

Unit 5

The events of a story are written in a certain order so the story makes sense.
Words like first, next, and last are used to help you follow the order.

Read each story. Draw a line from each event to show if it happened first, next, or last.

The first thing Tim does after school is eat a snack. His favorite snack is chocolate chip cookies and milk. Next, he plays with his dog, Toby. Tim and Toby play ball in the backyard. Last, Tim does his homework. He likes to finish his homework before dinner.

1. Tim does his homework.	First
2. Tim eats a snack.	Next
3. Tim plays with Toby.	Last

Meg and her family went camping. First, they set up the tent. Next, Meg and her dad went fishing. Meg caught two fish. Her dad caught one fish. Last, the whole family helped make dinner. They ate fish, corn, and rolls.

1. Meg and her dad went fishing.	First
2. The family set up the tent.	Next
3. Everyone helped to make dinner.	Last

Name

Sequencing with a diagram

Unit 5

A **diagram** is a picture or group of pictures showing the order of certain steps to an event. The pictures help make the steps easier to understand.

Example: 1. Dig a hole. 2. Plant some seeds. 3. Cover the seeds with dirt. 4. Water the seeds.

Cut out the pictures on page 72. Glue them in the correct order on the diagram.

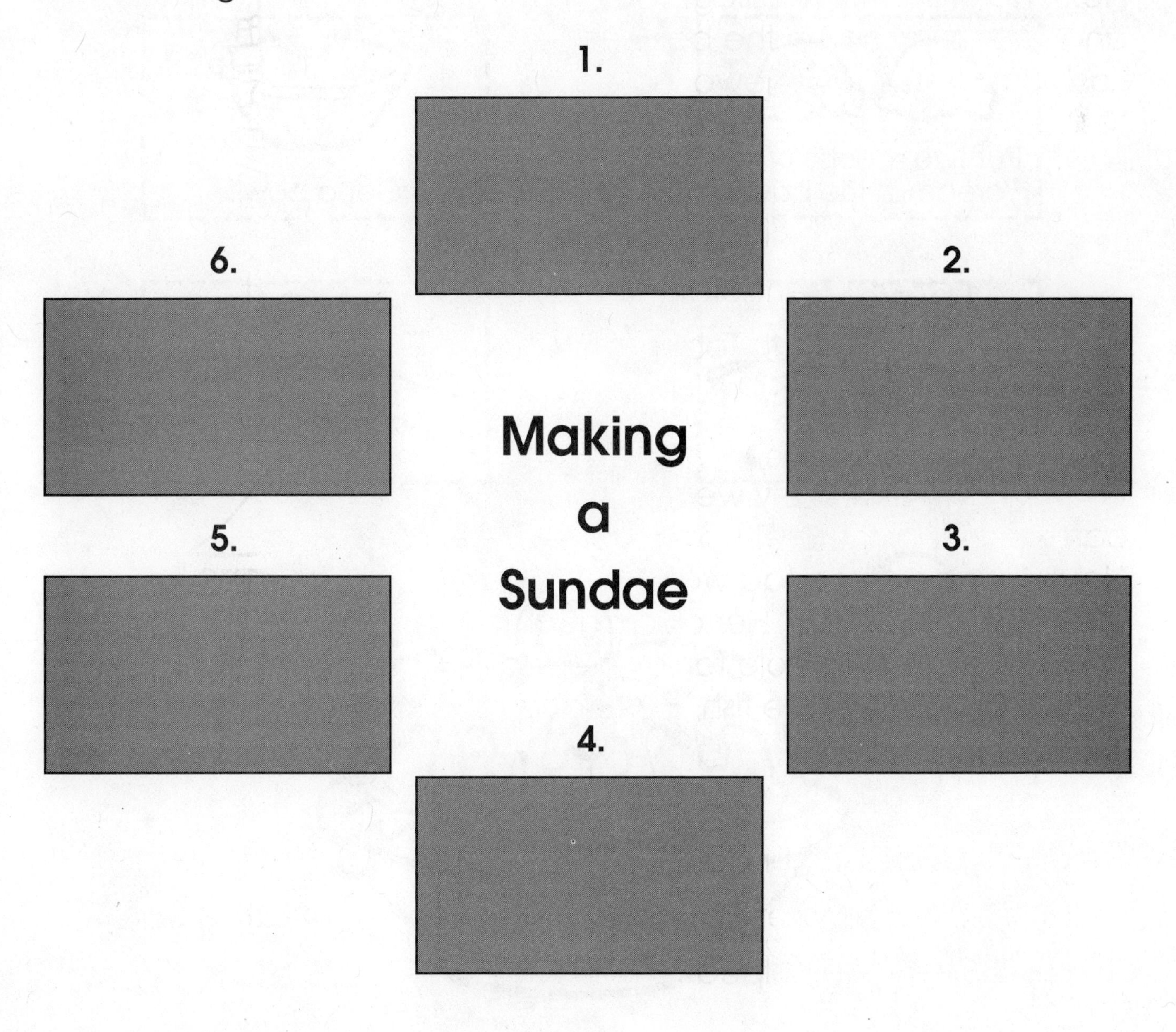

Name

Sequencing with a diagram (continued)

Unit 5

Squirt chocolate sauce over the ice cream.

Pour sprinkles over the chocolate sauce.

Put two scoops of ice cream in the bowl.

Get a bowl.

Eat the sundae.

Add a cherry to the top.

Name

Sequencing a story

Unit 5

The **sequence of a story** is the order the events in the story happened. To put a story in the correct order think about what happened first, second, and third.

Example:	Julie brushed her teeth.	Julie got into bed.	Julie fell asleep.
	1	2	3

Number the events in the order they happened.

1.

_____ Tanner's watch did not work in the morning.

_____ That evening Tanner bought a new watch.

_____ At noon Tanner tried to fix it.

2.

_____ Jack put two scoops of ice cream in the bowl.

_____ Jack got a bowl out of the cupboard.

_____ Jack put the empty bowl in the sink.

3.

_____ Nikki put on her raincoat.

_____ Nikki walked to the bus stop.

_____ Nikki watched the rain through the window.

4.

_____ Claire slid to the bottom.

_____ Claire ran to the slide.

_____ Claire climbed the ladder to the top.

Name

Sequencing a story — Unit 5

Longer stories have more events. To recall the events of the story it is important to keep the order of events in the correct sequence.

A Day at Wild City

The day was finally here. Ning and Lea were going to the Wild City Amusement Park. They had won tickets to the park by reading at school for 500 minutes.

Ning's mom, Mrs. Chan, drove the girls to the park. Mrs. Chan was going to the park, too. They all wore matching yellow shirts.

Ning chose the first ride. She chose the Crazy Loop Roller Coaster. It was her favorite ride. Next, Lea chose the Wacky Water Adventure. The girls took turns choosing rides all morning.

In the afternoon, they went to Marvin's Magic Show. They ate pink cotton candy and bubblegum ice cream. Before they went home, they each bought a yellow balloon.

Both girls fell asleep in the car on the way home. They were tired from all the fun.

Name

Sequencing a story (continued)

Unit 5

Number the story events from the story on page 74 in the order they happened.

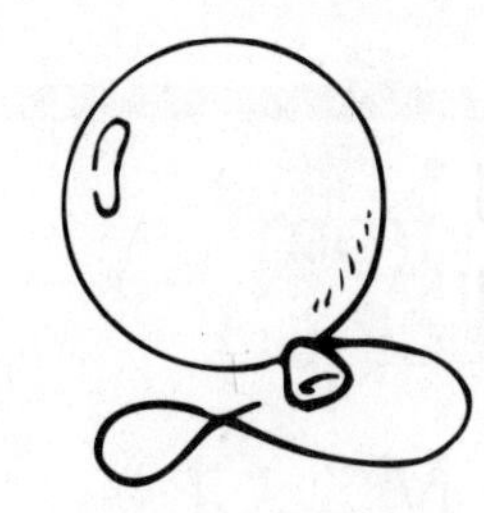

They went to Marvin's Magic Show.

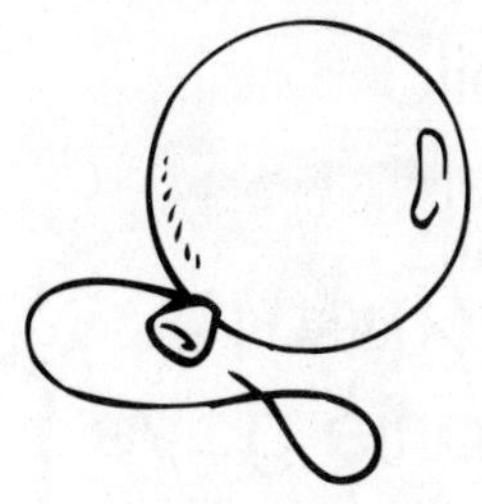

Ning and Lea fell asleep.

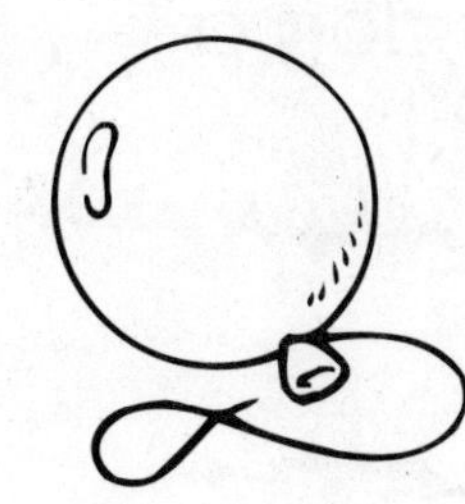

Ning and Lea won tickets to Wild City Amusement Park.

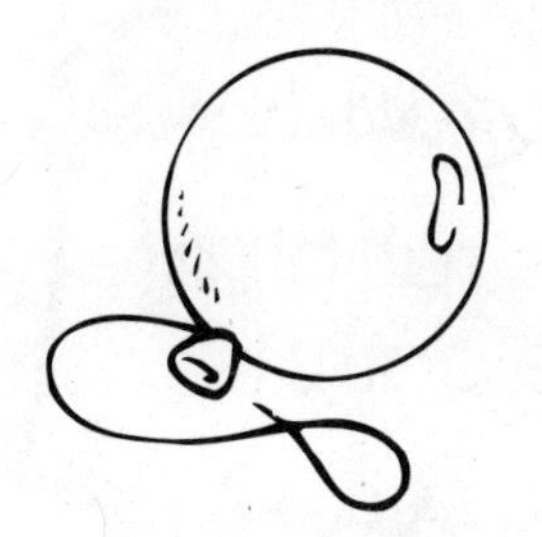

The girls rode the Crazy Loop Roller Coaster

Mrs. Chan drove Ning and Lea to the amusement park.

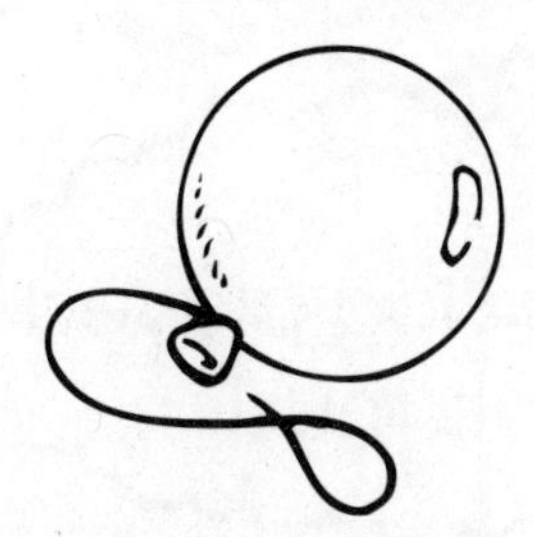

The girls bought yellow balloons.

Name

The cause of a story event

Unit 5

To help you understand a story better, an author often tells what made an event in the story happen. This is called the **cause**.

Example: In the story "The Three Little Pigs," the straw house of one pig is blown down. This happened because the wolf huffed and puffed and blew the house down. This is the cause.

Choose what made the events in the houses happen from the causes in the clouds below. Write the letter of the cloud above the correct house.

1. _____ Justin put on his hat and mittens.

2. _____ Sally put ice in the water.

3. _____ Charlie gave his dog a bath.

4. _____ Billy needed air in his bike tires.

5. _____ Kari got a new pair of shoes.

6. _____ The rabbit ate the carrot.

A. It was snowing outside.

B. Her feet had grown.

C. The bike tires were flat.

D. It was hungry.

E. The water was warm.

F. The dog played in the mud.

Name

Creating an effect

Unit 5

Sometimes in a story something makes something else happen. What happens is the **effect**, and what made it happen is the **cause**.

Example: In the book Where the Wild Things Are by Maurice Sendak (Harper Collins Children's Books, 1984), Max makes mischief and is sent to bed without dinner. What happens? Max imagines that he is king of all wild things. This is the effect.

Use your imagination to tell what happens for each cause.

1. Susie jumps in a puddle.

____

____

2. Ian forgets to shut the front door.

____

____

3. Nan leaves a book outside.

____

____

4. Andrew chases his sister.

____

____

Name

Unit 5 Test

Page 1

Sequencing, Cause and Effect

Read or listen to the directions. Fill in the circle beside the best answer.

❑ Example:

Read the story. What happens last?

I like to set the table. First, I set the cups on it. Then I set a spoon and fork at each place. Next, I set out the plates. Last, I put a napkin by each plate.

Watch for key words in the stories that give you clues.

Ⓐ I set the cups on the table.

Ⓑ I set a spoon and fork at each place.

Ⓒ I set out the plates.

Ⓓ I put a napkin by each plate.

Answer: D because this happened last.

Now try these. You have 25 minutes. Continue until you see .

1. Which picture happened first?

Name

Unit 5 Test

2. The Jets scored four goals. The Eagles scored two goals. The Jets won the soccer game.

Why did the Jets win?

(A) The Jets kicked the ball.
(B) The Jets are a good team.
(C) The Jets scored four goals.
(D) The Jets like to play soccer.

Use the diagram showing how to make lemonade to answer questions 3 and 4.

Pour mix into pitcher.

Fill pitcher with water.

Stir mix and water.

Pour into a glass.

3. What do you do last?

(A)

(B)

(C)

(D)

4. What do you do first?

(A)

(B)

(C)

(D)

GO ON

Name

Unit 5 Test

Page 3

Read the story to answer questions 5–8.

Mort the Mouse jumped out of bed. He had a busy day planned. First, he would let Tiger, the cat, chase him. Mort knew Tiger would never catch him. Tiger was too slow. Then he would go to the garden to find food. Mort hoped that the strawberries would be ripe. Next, Mort would take a nap. Last, Mort would fix a special dinner. His friend Timmy Toad was coming to eat with him.

5. What did Mort plan to do first?

Ⓐ let Tiger chase him
Ⓑ go to the garden
Ⓒ take a nap
Ⓓ fix dinner

6. What would Mort do after he went to the garden?

Ⓐ let Tiger chase him
Ⓑ go to the garden
Ⓒ take a nap
Ⓓ fix dinner

7. Mark the reason Mort was fixing dinner.

Ⓐ He liked strawberries.
Ⓑ He let Tiger chase him.
Ⓒ He jumped out of bed.
Ⓓ Timmy Toad was coming to dinner.

Name

Unit 5 Test

8. Why did Mort jump out of bed?

Ⓐ He had a busy day planned.
Ⓑ Tiger was chasing him.
Ⓒ He went to the garden.
Ⓓ He was making dinner.

9. Choose the picture that happened last.

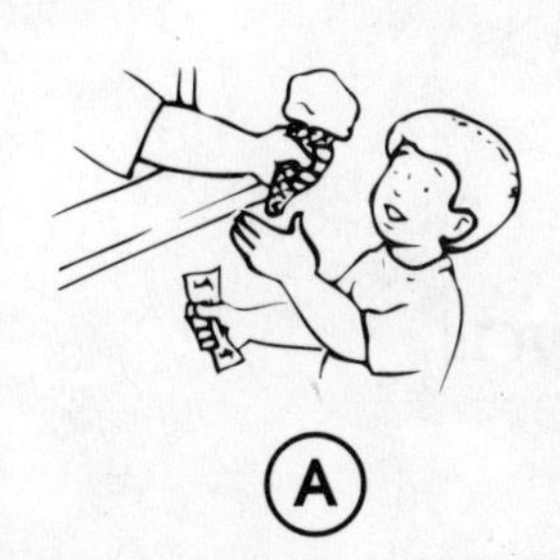
Ⓐ

Ⓑ

Ⓒ

Ⓓ

10. Read the nursery rhyme to answer the question.

It's raining, it's pouring,
The old man is snoring;
He got into bed
And bumped his head
And couldn't get up in the morning.

What happened because the man bumped his head?

Ⓐ It rained.
Ⓑ The man snored.
Ⓒ He got into bed.
Ⓓ He couldn't get up in the morning.

Name

Unit 5 Test

11. Mark what happened first.

Ⓐ Joey ate breakfast.
Ⓑ Joey got out of bed.
Ⓒ Joey rode the bus to school.
Ⓓ Joey played tag at recess.

12. Mark what happened last.

Ⓐ Tracy got crayons and paper.
Ⓑ Tracy gave the picture to her dad.
Ⓒ Tracy's dad put the picture on the wall.
Ⓓ Tracy drew a picture of her house.

13. Choose the picture that shows this step:
Put peanut butter on the bread.

Ⓐ

Ⓑ

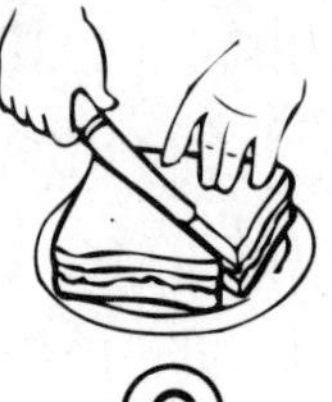
Ⓒ

Ⓓ

14. What would you do last?

Ⓐ Cut the sandwich in half.
Ⓑ Get peanut butter and bread.
Ⓒ Put peanut butter on the bread.
Ⓓ Eat the sandwich.

GO ON

Name

Unit 5 Test

Use the pictures to answer questions 15–18.

A. **B.** **C.** **D.**

15. What would happen first?

(A) (B) (C) (D)

16. Then what would happen?

(A) (B) (C) (D)

17. What would happen next?

(A) (B) (C) (D)

18. What would happen last?

(A) (B) (C) (D)

GO ON

Name

Unit 5 Test

Page 7

Read the story to answer questions 19 and 20.

Tad's grandmother gave him a new red ball. First, he played catch with Liam. Then he kicked it to his dog, Wolf. Next, he bounced it on the sidewalk. It started to rain. Tad went inside. He left the ball outside. The next day Tad could not find his ball.

19. What did Tad do first with his ball?

- (A) Tad played catch with Liam.
- (B) Tad kicked the ball to Wolf.
- (C) Tad bounced the ball on the sidewalk.
- (D) Tad left the ball outside.

20. What happened because Tad left his ball outside?

- (A) It rained.
- (B) He got a new ball.
- (C) He could not find it.
- (D) He bounced the ball on the sidewalk.

Put the sentences in the correct order.

I get out of the car.
My mom drives me to school.
I put on my seat belt.
I get into the car.

First, ______________________________

Then ______________________________

Next, ______________________________

Last, ______________________________

Name

Unit 6

Identifying characters

A **character** is a person or animal in a story.

Example: <u>Scott</u> rode the <u>whale</u> across the sea.
Scott and the whale are the characters.

Read the summary of <u>Arthur Goes to Camp</u> by Marc Brown (Little, Brown & Company, 1984). Underline the characters. Then circle the characters in the word find below. Names will go → and ↓ .

Arthur and his friends the Brain, Buster, and Francine left for Camp Meadowcroak. They rode in a bus. Muffy went to the camp, too. She rode there in a limo. Becky was the girls' camp leader. Rocky was the boys' camp leader. Arthur helped his team win the scavenger hunt.

L	M	A	F	R	A	N	C	I	N	E
B	U	S	T	E	R	B	N	E	I	T
E	F	C	P	Q	T	R	O	C	K	Y
C	F	R	D	G	H	M	Z	Y	K	O
K	Y	B	R	A	U	M	U	W	F	R
Y	V	E	B	B	R	A	I	N	X	J

Name

Character traits **Unit 6**

Character traits are the ways a character looks, acts, or feels.
You learn about a character through the sentences of the story.

A Day in the Garden

Sara and her friends worked in the garden. Sara wore a hat over her curly hair. Kip was very happy. He liked planting seeds. He wore his favorite shirt with lots of stars. Ali was tired and hot. She did not like working in the garden. Her sandals hurt her feet. Jack wore two different socks. He did not help. He played in the dirt.

Write the name of the character next to the correct picture.

Name

Understanding a character

Unit 6

A **character** shows his feelings and personality by what he says and does. This helps us better understand a character.

Example: Christina is crying.
We know Christina is sad because she is crying.

Circle the word that tells about the character.

1. Ted likes to tell jokes. He likes to make his friends laugh. Ted is a _______ person.

   sad funny shy

2. Andy covers his eyes. He does not like to watch lightning. Andy is _______ .

   proud sad afraid

3. Fran has many friends. She likes to help her teacher. Fran is a _______ person.

   funny nice shy

4. Juan smiles after the race. He wears his medal around his neck. Juan is _______ .

   silly proud shy

5. Max starts to yawn. He puts his head on his desk. Max is very _______.

   tired afraid silly

6. Teri cannot find her dog. She starts to cry. Teri is _______.

   happy proud sad

Name

Comparing characters

Unit 6

Stories with more than one character are fun to read because the characters are usually different from one another, just as the people you know are different.

The Twins

Kim and Kris are twins. They like to do a lot of the same things. They both like to jump rope, swim, and ride bikes.

But even twins like to do different things. Kim likes to play baseball, while Kris likes to dance. In the winter Kim likes to ice skate. Kris likes to go sledding. To help their mother, Kim sets the table. Kris sweeps the floor.

Both girls think it is fun to have a twin.

List three things Kim likes to do and three things Kris likes to do. Also list three things both girls like to do.

Kim

____

____

____

Kris

____

____

____

Both

____

____

____

Name

The setting

Unit 6

The **setting** tells where and when a story takes place. To figure out what the story's setting is, read the sentences carefully and look at the pictures.

Look at the pictures. Read the sentences. Draw a line from the picture to the sentences that describe it.

1\.

A. Troy plays by a pond. There are ducks swimming in the pond. Many trees grow near the pond.

2\.

B. There is a busy street near Carly's house. Many cars drive on the street. There is a bus stop in front of her house.

3\.

C. Kristen lives on a farm. A fence is in front of her house. A barn is next to her house.

4\.

D. Peter lives in a tall building. There is a park near the building. People walk their dogs in the park.

Name

Identifying the setting

Unit 6

The **setting** tells where and when a story takes place. Knowing where and when a story takes place helps you understand the story. To identify the setting ask yourself these questions: Where does the story take place? When does the story take place?

Write the setting from each sentence in the boxes. The letters in the dark boxes going down will answer the riddle.

What place in space is never hungry? ______________

1. The girls swam in the lake.
2. My grandmother lives in Afton.
3. Charlie's birthday is in June.
4. Gwen rode the train to the valley.
5. Jacob raked leaves in the fall.
6. The spaceship flew to Mars.
7. The party was on a boat.
8. My sister and I went to the zoo.
9. We had a picnic by the pond.

Name

The plot

Unit 6

The **plot** is the events that happen in a story. The plot is often divided into three parts: the beginning, middle, and end.

The pictures below each tell a story. Decide which part the picture tells: the **beginning**, **middle**, or **end**. Write which part on the line.

1.

______________ ______________ ______________

2.

______________ ______________ ______________

3.

______________ ______________ ______________

Name

Identifying the plot

Unit 6

The **plot** is the events that happen in a story. The character in a story often must solve a problem. The problem and how the character solves the problem are all part of the plot.

Example: In the fairy tale "Cinderella," Cinderella wants to go to the ball.
(This is the problem.)
Her fairy godmother helps her get to the ball.
(This is how the problem is solved.)
Both are part of the plot.

Read the stories. Answer the questions.

Maddie and her family went to the park for a picnic. They put a red blanket on the ground. Maddie's mom set the picnic basket on the blanket. Then they all went for a walk. When they returned there were hundreds of ants on the blanket. Maddie's dad grabbed the picnic basket. The family moved to a picnic table to enjoy their lunch.

1. What was the problem? ______________________________

____

2. How did Maddie's family solve the problem? __________

____

Today was the big race at Jackson's school. Jackson was excited about the race. He was a fast runner. He ran the fastest when he wore his black tennis shoes. After breakfast he went to his room to put on his black shoes. The shoes were not there. Where could they be? Jackson decided to ask everyone in his family if they had seen his shoes. He found his younger brother, Willy, wearing his shoes. Willy wanted to run fast, too.

3. What was the problem? ______________________________

____

4. How did Jackson solve the problem? ______________

____

Name

Developing a story

Unit 6

We have learned about the characters, setting, and plot of the story. They are all called the **story's elements**. Now let's put it all together.

Follow the steps below and on page 94 to plan a story of your own.

1. Plan two characters. Write their names and two words to describe them.

#1 ______________________________

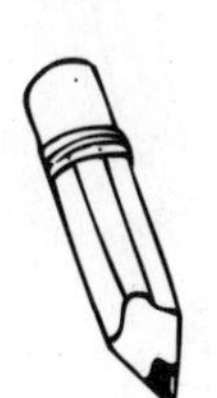
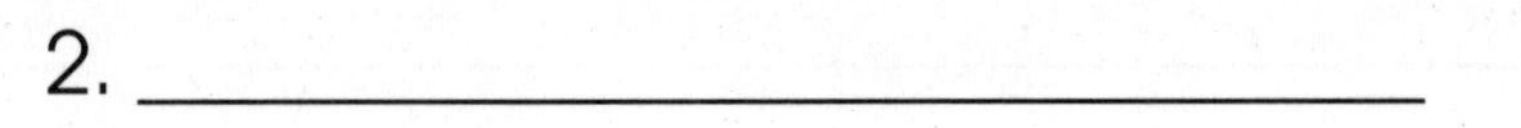

1. ______________________________

2. ______________________________

#2 ______________________________

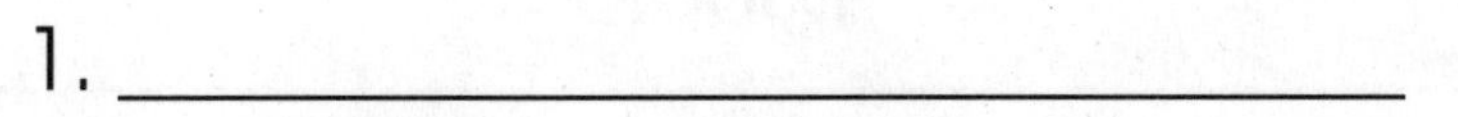
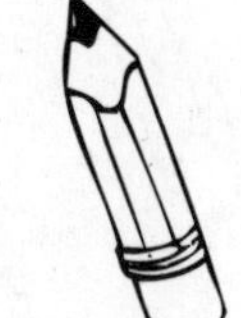

1. ______________________________

2. ______________________________

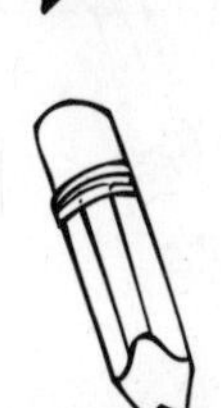
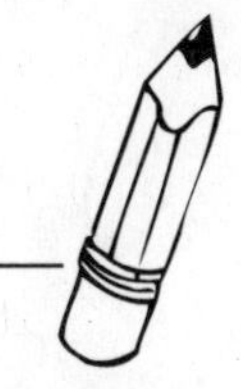

2. Where will your story take place? Write about your setting.

____

____

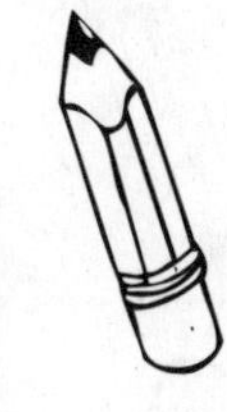

3. Draw a picture of your setting below.

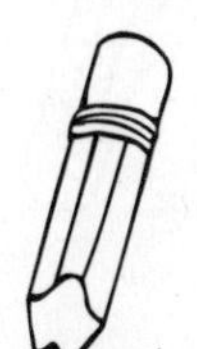

Name

Developing a story (continued)

Unit 6

4. Plan the beginning, middle, and end of your story.

Beginning

Middle

End

5. Turn your plan into a story or book! Use paper and pencil or a computer. Share your story with a friend.

Name

Unit 6 Test

Page 1

Story Elements

Read or listen to the directions. Fill in the circle beside the best answer.

- [ ] Example:

What is the setting in the story?

Wally the whale swam in the ocean. He wanted to play with one of his friends. Where could all his friends be?

Ⓐ Wally the whale
Ⓑ ocean
Ⓒ someone
Ⓓ friends

Fill in the circles neatly and completely.

Answer: B because it tells where the story takes place.

Now try these. You have 25 minutes. Continue until you see 
.

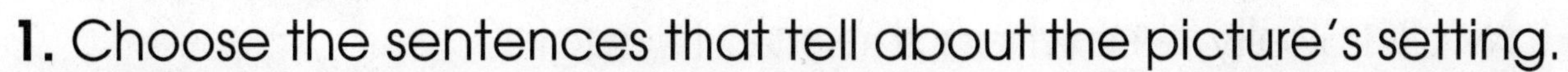

1. Choose the sentences that tell about the picture's setting.

Ⓐ There are many trees by Mara's house. Some of the trees are tall.

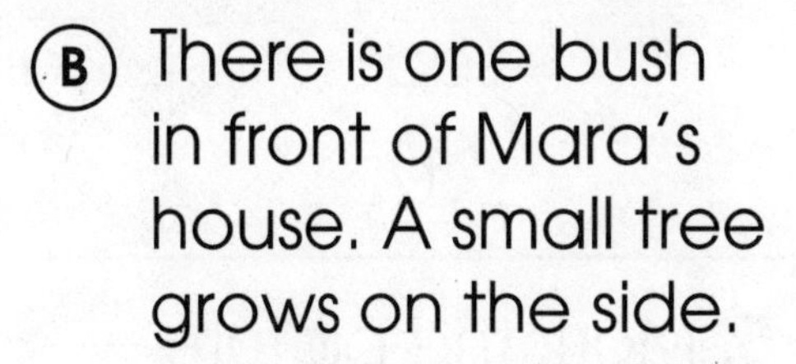

Ⓑ There is one bush in front of Mara's house. A small tree grows on the side.

Ⓒ There is a fence around Mara's house. Two trees grow in the front yard.

Ⓓ Mara's house is by the ocean. There is a beach near her house.

Name

Unit 6 Test

Read the story to answer questions 2–4.

Shelly could not find her lucky pencil. It helped her write the best stories. She looked all over her bedroom. The pencil was not under her bed. It was not on her table. Then Maggie, the dog, ran into the room. She had Shelly's pencil in her mouth. Shelly gave Maggie a big hug and kiss.

2. Choose the characters in the story.

Ⓐ room and bed Ⓑ Shelly and Maggie

Ⓒ hug and kiss Ⓓ pencil and stories

3. What is the setting of the story?

bedroom	pencil	Shelly	dog
Ⓐ	Ⓑ	Ⓒ	Ⓓ

4. How did Shelly feel when she saw Maggie?

sad	afraid	funny	happy
Ⓐ	Ⓑ	Ⓒ	Ⓓ

5. Mark the picture of the character.

Trent has short hair.
He wears glasses.
Trent is always happy.

GO ON

Name

Unit 6 Test

Read the story to answer questions 6 and 7.

Julie cried when she saw her bike. The bike had a flat tire. Julie's dad took the bike to the gas station. He pumped air into the tire. Now the tire was fixed. Julie rode her bike all afternoon.

6. How did Julie feel at the beginning of the story?

sad	proud	shy	happy
(A)	(B)	(C)	(D)

7. What was the problem in the story?

(A) Julie saw her bike.
(B) Julie's bike had a flat tire.
(C) Julie's dad fixed the tire.
(D) Julie rode her bike.

8. Choose the picture that shows the setting.

Lisa flew to the moon.
She collected moon dust in a bag.

(A)

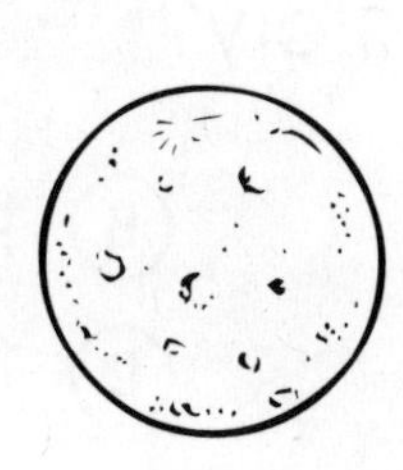
(B)

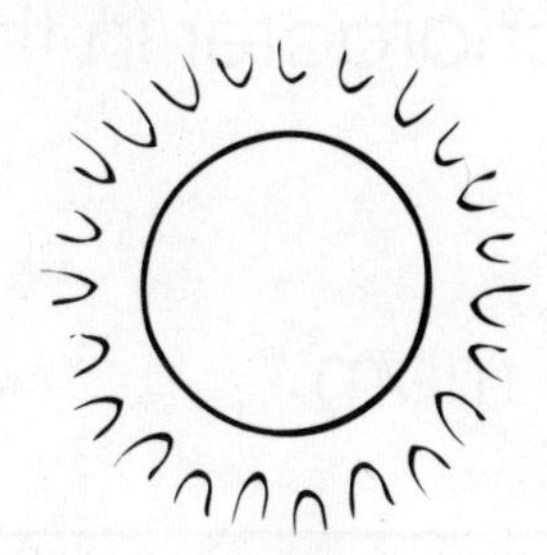
(C)

(D)

GO ON

Name

Unit 6 Test

Read the story to answer questions 9–12.

Will's family was planning a vacation. Will wanted to go to the mountains. He liked to hike and ski. His sister, Kristen, wanted to go to the beach. She liked to swim and collect shells. They both liked to fish. Their mom had an idea. She said they should go to the lake. Will could waterski, and Kristen could swim. The whole family could fish. Both Will and Kristen thought that would be a great vacation!

9. What do both Will and Kristen like to do?

hike	swim	fish	ski
(A)	(B)	(C)	(D)

10. Choose what happens at the beginning of the story.

(A) Will went hiking.
(B) The family went fishing.
(C) Their mom had an idea.
(D) The family was planning a vacation.

11. Who is not a character in the story?

(A) Will
(B) Kristen
(C) the mom
(D) fish

Name

Unit 6 Test

12. How are Will and Kristen different?

Ⓐ Will likes to hike. Kristen likes to ski.
Ⓑ Will likes to fish. Kristen does not like to fish.
Ⓒ Will likes to ski. Kristen likes to swim.
Ⓓ Will likes the beach. Kristen likes the mountains.

13. Which picture shows the plot of a story?

Ⓐ

Ⓑ

Ⓒ

Ⓓ

14. Who is a character in the story?

It was a beautiful day! Sam was playing in the sandbox. Taylor and Emily were playing at the park. Tom was at the baseball field. They were all having fun.

Ⓐ Sam
Ⓑ the sandbox
Ⓒ playing
Ⓓ Todd

GO ON

Name

Unit 6 Test

Read the story to answer questions 15–17.

Larry saw Mittens, the cat, on the roof. Mittens could not get down. Larry's dad got a ladder. He climbed the ladder. He carried Mittens to the ground.

15. How did Mittens probably feel at the beginning of the story?

scared	brave	silly	tired
Ⓐ	Ⓑ	Ⓒ	Ⓓ

16. Which sentence tells about the middle of the story?

Ⓐ Larry saw Mittens on the roof.
Ⓑ Larry's dad climbed the ladder.
Ⓒ He carried Mittens to the ground.
Ⓓ Mittens felt safe.

17. What was the problem?

Ⓐ Larry saw Mittens.
Ⓑ Larry's dad got a ladder.
Ⓒ Mittens could not get down from the roof.
Ⓓ Larry's dad carried Mittens.

GO ON

Name

Unit 6 Test

Read the story to answer questions 18–20.

Susan and Carol like to draw. Susan draws pictures of animals. Her favorite animal is a lion. Carol likes to draw people. She draws every day. Susan uses crayons when she draws. Carol uses colored pencils.

18. How are the two girls the same?

Ⓐ They draw animals.
Ⓑ They draw people.
Ⓒ They use crayons.
Ⓓ They like to draw.

19. Which picture did Susan not draw?

Ⓐ

Ⓑ

Ⓒ

Ⓓ

20. Which sentence tells about Carol?

Ⓐ She likes to draw animals.
Ⓑ Her favorite animal is a lion.
Ⓒ She likes to draw people.
Ⓓ She draws with crayons.

Write a sentence that tells about the setting of a story.

____

____

Name

Predicting outcomes using pictures

Unit 7

To **predict** is to use clues from a story or picture to guess what will happen next.

Draw a picture showing what you think will happen next.

1.

2.

3.

Name

Predicting story events

Unit 7

There are often clues hidden in a story that give you an idea of what will happen next.

Read the story below and on page 104. Circle the correct answers to the questions.

It is cold outside. Snow is falling. Jan and Jill want to go sledding on the hill in the backyard. Jill is ready to go. Jan grabs her coat but runs back inside?

1. What has Jan forgotten?

her backpack   her hat and mittens   a beach towel

The girls each pull a sled to the top of the hill. Jill wants to have a race. Jan and Jill jump on their sleds. Jan races down the hill. Jill's sled is stuck.

2. Who will win the race?

Jan   Jill   both girls

Next, the girls make three giant snowballs. They set one snowball on top of the biggest snowball. They set the smallest snowball on the very top. Jan goes inside to get a hat and scarf. Jill looks for two sticks.

3. What are the girls making?

a scarecrow   a snow fort   a snowman

Name

Predicting story events (continued)

Unit 7

The sidewalk was covered with snow. The girls each grabbed a shovel. They began to shovel the snow off the sidewalk. It was hard work! There was ice under the snow on the sidewalk. It was slippery. Jill ran across the sidewalk. Oops!

4. What happened to Jill?

She fell down.   She got wet.   She went inside.

The girls are tired and cold. They put their shovels in the garage. Then they go inside to get something warm to drink.

5. What will they drink?

lemonade   hot chocolate   ice water

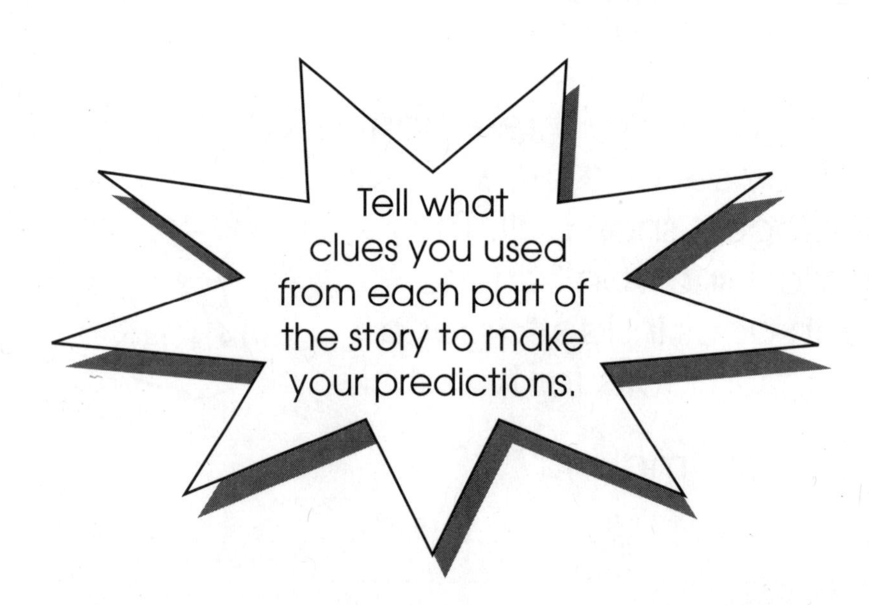

Name

Predicting story outcomes

Unit 7

The things the characters in a story say or do are clues about what might happen next in the story. Thinking about what will happen in a story helps you to better understand the story.

Write a sentence to tell what you think will happen next.

Morgan the monkey wanted to play. She climbed a tree looking for her friend Mabel. "Mabel is not here," Mabel's mom said. "She is playing with Mombo by the river."

1. What will Morgan do? ______________________________

____

The three monkeys played by the river. They liked to run and chase each other. Mombo was the fastest. He always caught Mabel and Morgan. They decided to have a race.

2. Who will win? ______________________________

____

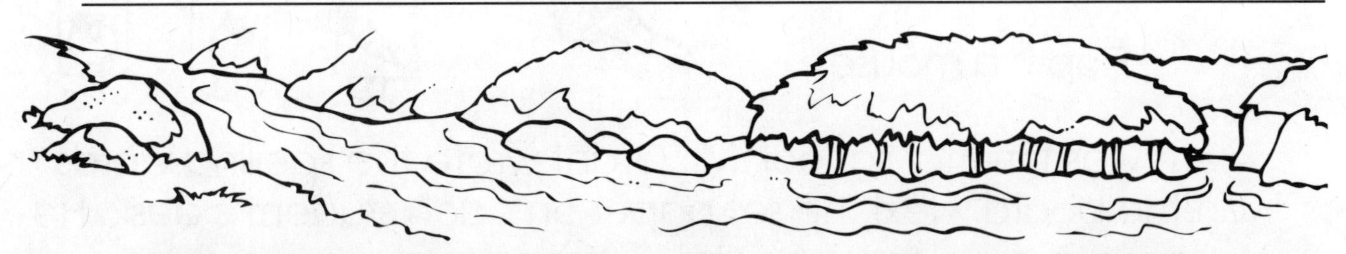

Morgan, Mabel, and Mombo were tired from running. They all liked to take a nap in the afternoon. The three monkeys climbed a tree. They swung from tree to tree back home.

3. Now what will the monkeys do? ______________________

____

Name

Predicting a character Unit 7

You can make predictions or guesses about characters using clues from the story.

Use clues from the stories to make guesses about the characters. Circle the correct answers.

It was time to get ready for the party. Kara put on a new dress. The dress was yellow with pink flowers. Kara's mom tied a pink ribbon in Kara's hair. Kara was excited!

1. Who is Kara?

   Kara is a boy.

   Kara is a cat.

   Kara is a girl.

Flop hopped to the garden. Flop was hungry. Someone had pulled two carrots out of the dirt. Flop ate both carrots.

2. Who is Flop?

   Flop is a dog.

   Flop is a rabbit.

   Flop is a mouse.

It was time for school. Mr. Grant wrote the spelling words on the board. Next, he set paper on each student's desk. He was ready for class to begin.

3. Who is Mr. Grant?

   Mr. Grant is a teacher.

   Mr. Grant is a policeman.

   Mr. Grant is a doctor.

Name

Drawing conclusions

Unit 7

Sometimes the events in a story help you form opinions or ideas about the story. This is called **drawing conclusions**. The answer to some questions may or may not be in the story, but by reading carefully, you will have an idea about what the answer might be.

Fill in the circles that best tell about the sentences.

1. Carter's family is watching a movie. They are all laughing.

   Ⓐ They do not like the movie.

   Ⓑ The movie is funny.

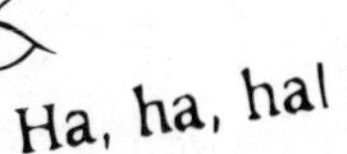

2. Juan jumps off the bus. He runs inside to get a snack.

   Ⓐ Juan is coming home from school.

   Ⓑ It is time for dinner.

3. Karen helps her mom put clothes in the suitcase. Her dad fills the car with gas.

   Ⓐ They are having a party.

   Ⓑ They are going on vacation.

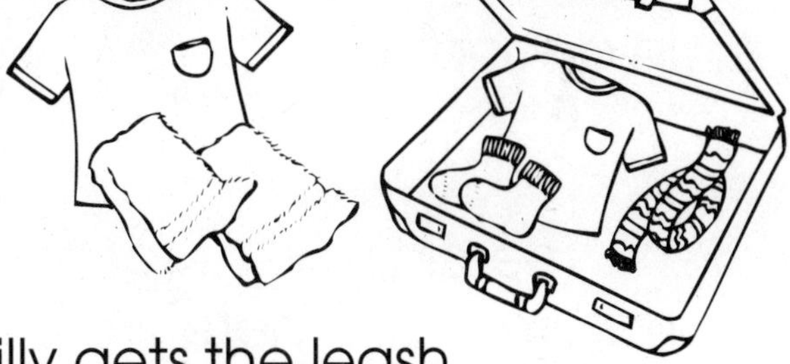

4. Lilly's dog is barking at the door. Lilly gets the leash.

   Ⓐ Lilly and the dog will go for a walk.

   Ⓑ Lilly and the dog will go to sleep.

5. The mouse runs across the floor. It sees a piece of cheese.

   Ⓐ The mouse will jump over the cheese.

   Ⓑ The mouse will eat the cheese.

Name

Predicting a setting

Unit 7

Sometimes an author does not tell you where the setting is. You can make predictions or guesses about the setting using clues from the story.

Circle the correct settings using clues from the stories.

1. Alexa liked to swim in the ocean. Diving in the waves was so much fun! Her brother liked to dig holes in the sand. Alexa and her brother built a sandcastle. Their mother took a picture of it.

   Where were they?

   on a beach

   at a swimming pool

   in a sandbox

2. Joey rode the tractor with his grandfather. It was big and green. Next, he helped his grandmother feed the chickens. Then they picked green beans. Later, they all rode horses. It was a busy day!

   Where were they?

   at a zoo

   in a town

   on a farm

3. The class went for a nature walk. There were many tall trees. They saw a deer run around the trees. They collected many nuts and leaves.

   Where were they?

   in a garden

   in a forest

   in a backyard

4. Tom jumped off the diving board. He made a big splash. Then he tried to dive. He landed on his stomach. Boy, did that hurt!

   Where was he?

   in a swimming pool

   in a pond

   in a ocean

Name

Fact and opinion Unit 7

A **fact** is something that you know is true.
An **opinion** is what you believe about something.
Example: Mr. Greene is a teacher. (This is a fact.)
Mr. Greene is the best teacher. (This is an opinion.)

Get the rocket to the moon.
Color the stars blue that tell a fact.

Name

Unit 7 Test

Page 1

Predicting, Drawing Conclusions, Recognizing Fact vs. Opinion

Read or listen to the directions. Fill in the circle beside the best answer.

☐ Example:

Choose the fact.

Ⓐ Apples grow on trees.

Ⓑ Apple juice is the best drink.

Ⓒ Apple pie is great.

Ⓓ Apples are the tastiest fruit.

Use your time wisely. If a question seems too tough, skip it and come back to it later.

Answer: A because this is always true.

Now try these. You have 25 minutes. Continue until you see .

1. Mark the picture that shows what will happen next.

Ⓐ Ⓑ Ⓒ Ⓓ

GO ON

Name

Unit 7 Test

Use the clues in the stories to answer questions 2–10.

2. The game was over. The team yelled, "Three cheers for Jim!"

What probably happened?

Ⓐ Jim went to school.

Ⓑ Jim forgot the game.

Ⓒ Jim scored a goal.

Ⓓ The team ate dinner.

3. Scott was waiting for the bus. He did not have his library book. Scott went back inside the house.

Why did Scott go back inside?

Ⓐ He missed the bus.

Ⓑ He was hungry.

Ⓒ He needed a pencil.

Ⓓ He needed to get his library book.

4. Many children rode to school with Miss Baker every day. She took the same children home in the afternoon. Miss Baker liked her job.

Who is Miss Baker?

Ⓐ She is a teacher.

Ⓑ She is a bus driver.

Ⓒ She is a doctor.

Ⓓ She is a secretary.

Name

Unit 7 Test

5. Tina wants a bike for her birthday. Tina's dad buys her a present. He cannot put it in a box. It is too big. He knows Tina will like her present.

What is the present?

a book	a doll	a bike	a dress
Ⓐ	Ⓑ	Ⓒ	Ⓓ

6. Both teams were ready to play. The fans sat in the bleachers. The umpire yelled, "Batter up!"

Where does the story take place?

Ⓐ a baseball field
Ⓑ at school
Ⓒ at home
Ⓓ a playground

7. Andy and his family got in the car. They were going to visit their grandma. She lived three hours away. The gas tank was empty.

What will they do next?

Ⓐ Eat a snack.
Ⓑ Pack their suitcases.
Ⓒ Go to Grandma's house.
Ⓓ Go to the gas station.

GO ON

Name

Unit 7 Test

8. Raja lives at a zoo. He uses his long trunk to eat and drink. His gray skin is wrinkled.

What is Raja?

(A) a wolf
(B) an elephant
(C) a lion
(D) a turtle

9. Susie likes to paint flowers. She wants to paint a picture for her dad. Her friend Joan has a flower garden. Susie takes her paints to Joan's house.

What will Susie do?

(A) Play with Joan.
(B) Pick some flowers.
(C) Paint a flower picture.
(D) Go home with her dad.

10. Kevin likes to shop with his mom. Kevin pushes the cart. His mom picks out food to put in the cart.

Where is Kevin?

(A) a toy store
(B) a grocery store
(C) home
(D) school

GO ON

Name

Unit 7 Test

11. Mark the picture that shows what will happen next.

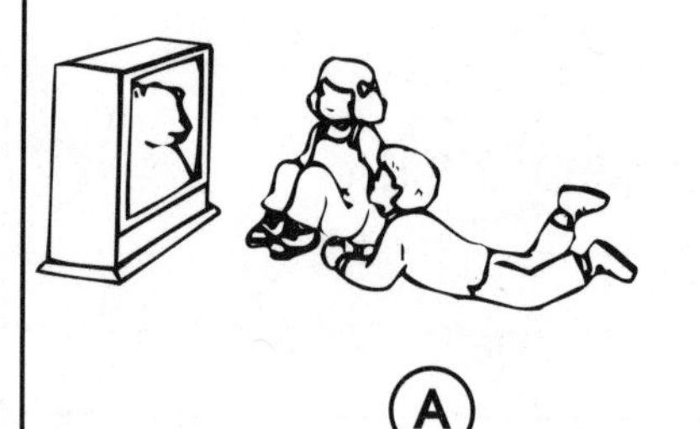

(A) (B) (C) (D)

12. Choose the fact.

(A) Fish are fun to watch.
(B) Fish are the best pets.
(C) Fish do not smell good.
(D) Fish live in water.

Read the story to answer questions 13 and 14.

It was a warm fall day. Mrs. Kane takes her class to the park. The class is going on a nature walk. They will look at the colorful trees. Each student has a small paper bag to collect things.

13. What will they put in the bags?

leaves	lunch	seashells	pencils
(A)	(B)	(C)	(D)

GO ON

Name

Unit 7 Test

14. They walk for an hour. Now the students are hungry. Mrs. Kane has a surprise for the class.

What is the surprise?

a tree	an animal	a ball	a snack
Ⓐ	Ⓑ	Ⓒ	Ⓓ

15. Which is not a fact?

Ⓐ The house is white.

Ⓑ The house has a red door.

Ⓒ It is the best house.

Ⓓ There are two trees in the yard.

Write a fact about your school.

____

____

Name

Final Review Test

Page 1

Read or listen to the directions. Fill in the circle beside the best answer.

❑ Example:

Choose the sentence that could not really happen.

Ⓐ We saw the lion at the zoo.
Ⓑ The lion roared.
Ⓒ The lion drove the train.
Ⓓ The lion was hungry.

Answer: C because a lion cannot drive a train.

Now try these. You have 30 minutes.

Continue until you see  .

Remember your Helping Hand Strategies:

1. Watch for key words in the stories that give you clues.

2. Fill in the circles neatly and completely.

3. Use your time wisely. If a question seems too tough, skip it and come back to it later.

1. Which letter makes the middle sound in  ?

a	e	i	o
Ⓐ	Ⓑ	Ⓒ	Ⓓ

2. Which word means the same as **small**?

ball	smell	huge	little
Ⓐ	Ⓑ	Ⓒ	Ⓓ

Name

Final Review Test

3. Choose the word that does not belong.

wet	lake	pond	river
(A)	(B)	(C)	(D)

Read the story to answer questions 4–7.

José's mom drove him to school in her car. José was very excited. Today was a special day! His school was having a birthday party. The school was 10 years old. First, all the students would march in a parade. Then, they would have a picnic. Next, they would sing "Happy Birthday" and eat birthday cake. What a fun day it would be!

4. Choose the best title for the story.

(A) The Parade
(B) The School's Birthday
(C) José at Recess
(D) The School Picnic

5. How did José get to school?

(A) He rode a bus.
(B) He walked.
(C) He rode in a car.
(D) He rode his bike.

GO ON

Name

Final Review Test

Page 3

6. What will happen last at the birthday party?

Ⓐ There will be a parade.
Ⓑ The students will sing "Happy Birthday."
Ⓒ José will open presents.
Ⓓ There will be a long recess.

7. Why is José excited?

Ⓐ It was a special day at school.
Ⓑ His mom drove him to school.
Ⓒ He ate birthday cake.
Ⓓ He played at recess.

Read the story to answer questions 8 and 9.

Caleb and his family are riding in a boat on the river. His dad steers the boat. His sister, Susan, skis behind the boat. Later, they will stop the boat and swim.

8. Who is not a character in the story?

Ⓐ Caleb
Ⓑ Susan
Ⓒ the river
Ⓓ Caleb's dad

Name

Final Review Test

Page 4

9. Choose the picture that shows the setting.

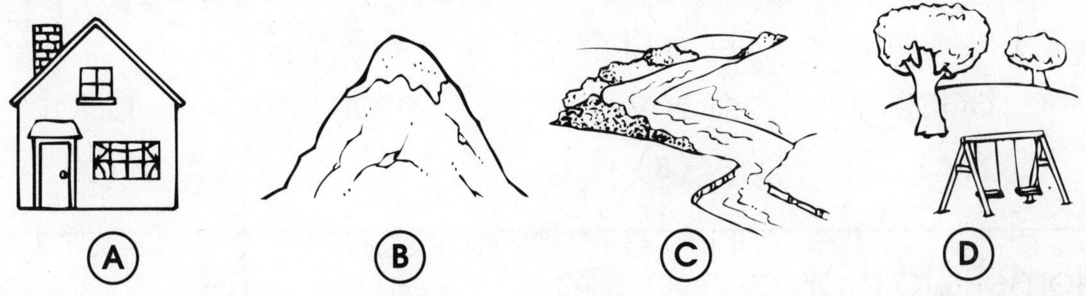

(A) (B) (C) (D)

10. Alex did not like to wear shoes. He could not wiggle his toes. He could run faster without shoes. Alex walked to the bus stop. His friends started to laugh. "Alex, didn't you forget something?" someone asked.

What did Alex forget?

(A) his shoes (B) his backpack
(C) his lunch (D) his coat

11. Mark the picture that shows what would happen next.

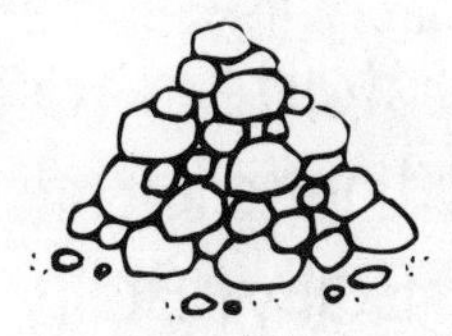

(A) (B) (C) (D)

GO ON

Name

Final Review Test

Page 5

12. Which word has the same ending sound as 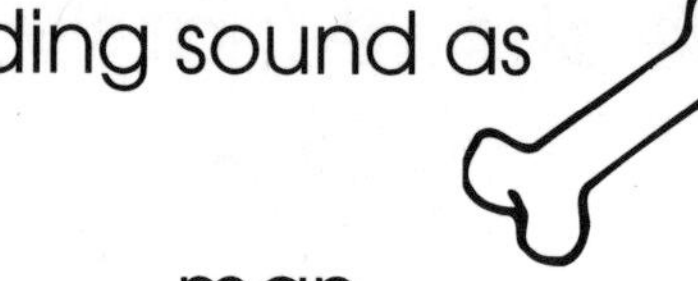 ?

book	tiny	man	boat
(A)	(B)	(C)	(D)

13. Home is to man as nest is to _____.

bird	egg	sticks	tree
(A)	(B)	(C)	(D)

14. Which word comes first in alphabetical order?

goat	car	fox	bike
(A)	(B)	(C)	(D)

Read the story to answer questions 15–18.

"Rita, I have a surprise for you," her father said.

"What is it?" Rita asked.

"A magic bike. It will take you wherever you want to go."

Rita was very excited. She got on her new bike and started to pedal. Before she knew it, she was riding through the clouds. She saw a pretty bird. The bird's name was Bally. Bally sat on Rita's arm. Bally and Rita became friends. Next, Rita saw an orange butterfly. The butterfly landed on Rita's head. Bally, Rita, and the butterfly rode to a star. They played all day on the star.

GO ON

Name

Final Review Test

15. Choose the best title for the story.

- Ⓐ Rita and Her Father
- Ⓑ The Butterfly
- Ⓒ The Magic Bike
- Ⓓ Playing on a Star

16. What could really happen?

- Ⓐ Rita rides her bike through a cloud.
- Ⓑ Rita pedals her bike.
- Ⓒ Rita plays on a star.
- Ⓓ Rita gets a magic bike.

17. Choose the picture that shows the setting.

Ⓐ Ⓑ Ⓒ Ⓓ

18. What happens first in the story?

Ⓐ Ⓑ Ⓒ Ⓓ

GO ON

Name

Final Review Test

19. The book is all wet.

Why might this happen?

- (A) The book is outside. It starts to rain.
- (B) The book is at school.
- (C) The book is about rain.
- (D) That is my favorite book.

20. Which picture shows the plot of a story?

(A) (B) (C) (D)

21. It is very hot. The girls are playing outside. They want to cool off. Mother has an idea. She gets their swimsuits and towels.

What will the girls do?

- (A) Water the flowers.
- (B) Go inside.
- (C) Play a game.
- (D) Go to the swimming pool.

GO ON

Name

Final Review Test

22. What two letters make the beginning sound in  ?

ch (A) sh (B) ce (C) ee (D)

23. Mark the word that completes the sentence.

He won a _____ at the race.

meal (A) melt (B) medal (C) march (D)

24. Draw a square.
Write **dog** above the square.
Draw a circle inside the square.

Choose the picture that matches the directions.

dog

(A)

dog

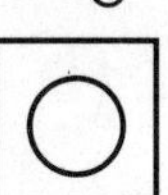

(B)

dog

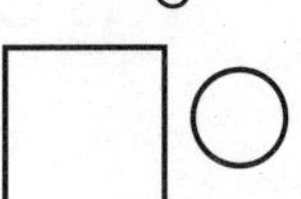

(C)

dog

(D)

GO ON

Name

Final Review Test

Page 9

Read the story to answer questions 25–27.

Harry and Matt went outside to play baseball. They played in their backyard. Justin and Dan came to play, too. Matt threw the ball to Dan. Dan swung the bat. He missed the ball. Matt threw the ball again. Dan hit the ball hard. It flew over Matt's head. All the boys yelled, "Oh, no!" The ball was heading toward a window.

25. What do you think will happen?

- (A) Dan will hit a home run.
- (B) Matt will catch the ball.
- (C) Justin will throw the ball.
- (D) The ball will hit a window.

26. Where does this story take place?

- (A) a baseball field
- (B) a house
- (C) a backyard
- (D) a school

27. What happened in the middle of the story?

- (A) Harry and Matt went outside to play.
- (B) A window broke.
- (C) The ball head towards a window.
- (D) Dan hit the ball.

Name

Final Review Test

28. What word rhymes with  ?

town (A) cow (B) clean (C) slow (D)

29. Choose a title for the picture.

(A) The Egg Cracks
(B) The Snake Hatches
(C) The Jungle Snake
(D) A Garden Snake

30. Mark the word that means the opposite of **best**.

test (A) worst (B) great (C) begin (D)

A turtle is a reptile. They live almost everywhere. They cannot live where it is cold all year. Sea turtles are the fastest. Turtles have no teeth. They have a beak to cut food. Turtles are interesting to study.

Write a title for the story. ______________________

Write two facts from the story. ______________________

____

____

STOP

Answer Key

Page 5

1. f; 2. b; 3. v; 4. q; 5. j; 6. n; 7. h; 8. d; 9. l; 10. p; 11. z; 12. r; 13. k; 14. t; 15. m; 16. d

Page 6

1. q; 2. n; 3. b; 4. k; 5. h; 6. r; 7. d; 8. x; 9. t; 10. f; 11. l; 12. p

Page 7

1. cow; 2.sad; 3. circle; 4. cage; 5. cent; 6. magic; 7. grass; 8. rose; 9. square

Page 8

1. cup; 2. dot; 3. leg; 4. fan; 5. mop; 6. lips; 7. pig; 8. net; 9. hat; 10. truck

Page 9

1. wave; 2. bike; 3. nine; 4. home; 5. bone; 6. dime; 7. hole; 8. kite; 9. tire; 10. lake

Page 10

1. child; 2. whale; 3. catch; 4. ship; 5. wish; 6. thumb

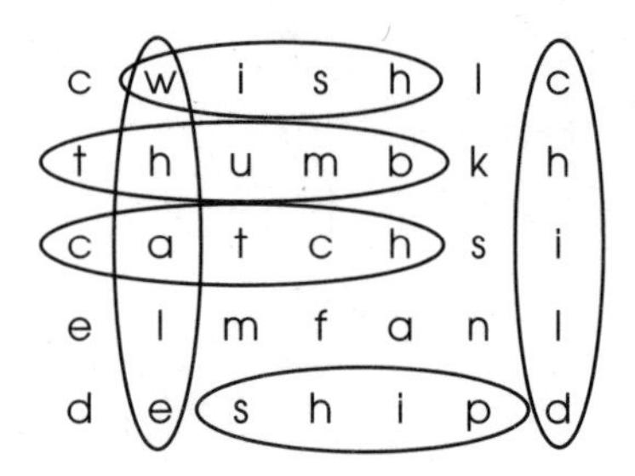

Page 11

1. tree; 2. sled; 3. cloud; 4. flame; 5. snake; 6. plate; 7. twenty; 8. swim; 9. smoke; 10. skate; 11. steps; 12. brush

Page 12

1. sleep; 2. rain; 3. soap; 4. pail; 5. boat; 6. beach; 7. see

Page 13

baby: city, lady, easy, party; cry: by, why, try, shy; 1. snow; 2. hay; 3. play; 4. slow; 5. blow; 6. tray

Page 14

1. car; 2. first; 3. fur; 4. birds; 5. after; 6. dark; 7. stars

Unit 1 Test

1. B; 2. A; 3. D; 4. C; 5. A; 6. C; 7. C; 8. D; 9. B; 10. B; 11. A; 12. D; 13. C; 14. B; 15. A; 16. C; 17. D; 18. B; 19. D; 20. A; Constructed-response answers will vary.

Page 20

1. can; 2. two; 3. three; 4. tent; 5. shop; 6. day; 7. brown; 8. boy; 9. kiss

Page 21

1. bathtub; 2. butterfly; 3. sunglasses; 4. popcorn; 5. cowboy; 6. starfish; 7. grandmother; 8. skateboard; 9. bedtime

Page 22

1. cap; 2. place; 3. quick; 4. keep; 5. kind; 6. sleep; 7. run; 8. choose

Page 23

1. night; 2. short; 3. little; 4. cold; 5. new; 6. under

Page 24

1. saw; 2. fall; 3. star; 4. roll; 5. back

Page 25

1. desk; 2. flowers; 3. shoes; 4. teeth; 5. cheese; 6. hole; 7. child; 8. tail; 9. break; 10. tree; 11. window; 12. chair

Page 26

1. soap; 2. rabbit; 3. seeds; 4. cloud; 5. bikes; 6. clean; 7. party; 8. under

Page 27

1. banana; 2. bike; 3. over; 4. ball; 5. sled; 6. fish; 7. head; 8. hear; 9. cold

Page 28

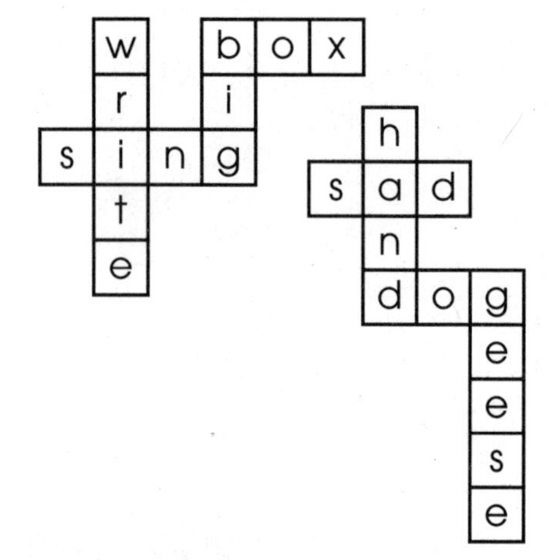

Unit 2 Test

1. B; 2. C; 3. A; 4. B; 5. D; 6. A; 7. C; 8. C; 9. D; 10. A; 11. A; 12. B; 13. C; 14. A; 15. A; 16. B; 17. C; 18. B; 19. D; 20. B; Constructed-response answers will vary.

Answer Key

Page 34

Check students' drawings.

Page 35

Check students' drawings.

Page 36

1. farm animals; 2. things that go; 3. things to eat; 4. shapes; 5. pets; 6. tools

Page 37

1. dog; 2. car; 3. toys; 4. girl; 5. paper; 6. sit

Page 38

1. T, V, Y; 2. h, j, o; 3. d, e, h; 4. m, p, s; 5. c, f, i; 6. g, n, q; 7. s, t, w; 8. b, h, n; 9. o, u, y; 10. h, i, l; They swim in schools.

Page 39

1. can, man, tan; 2. grass, sky, tree; 3. four, nine, one; 4. blue, pink, red; 5. crab, frog, shell; 6. fox, lion, wolf

Page 40

Answers will vary.

Page 41

1. A Bat's Wings; 2. 4; 3. 4; 4. 1; 5. 2; 6. 3; 7. 15

Unit 3 Test

1. C; 2. A; 3. C; 4. B; 5. C; 6. A; 7. C; 8. B; 9. A; 10. D; 11. B; 12. C; 13. A; 14. B; 15. D; 16. B; 17. B; 18. A; 19. B; 20. D; Constructed-response answers will vary.

Page 48

1. My Pet Fish; 2. A Trip to the Moon; 3. Fun at the Pool; 4. A Bird Adventure; 5. I'm All Wet!; 6. The Cat Picture; 7. Answers will vary.

Page 49

1. A Wish Before Bed; 2. The Turtle Dream; 3. The Sleepover; 4. A New Puppy

Page 50

1. B; 2. C; 3. A

Page 51

1. seven; 2. pancakes; 3. Tara's house; 4. grilled cheese sandwiches and watermelon; 5. chocolate cake with white icing

Page 52

1. Jack and Joe; 2. 25¢; 3. 2; 4. 2 times around the block; 5. weed pulling

Page 53

1. habitat; 2. a creek near some woods; 3. insects; 4. quiet; 5. need to live

Page 54

Colored turtles should be 2, 3, and 5.

Page 55

1. blue/fantasy; 2. yellow/real; 3. yellow/real; 4. blue/fantasy; 5. blue/fantasy; 6. blue/fantasy; 7. yellow/real; 8. blue/fantasy; 9. blue/fantasy; 10. yellow/real; 11. blue/fantasy

Unit 4 Test

1. D; 2. D; 3. C; 4. A; 5. D; 6. B; 7. D; 8. B; 9. C; 10. C; 11. A; 12. C; 13. B; 14. A; 15. A; 16. C; 17. D; 18. D; 19. B; 20. C; Constructed-response answers will vary.

Midway Review Test

1. B; 2. C; 3. A; 4. C; 5. A; 6. B; 7. C; 8. B; 9. D; 10. A; 11. B; 12. A; 13. B; 14. C; 15. D; 16. A; 17. B; 18. B; 19. D; 20. C; Constructed-response answers will vary.

Page 69

1. 2, 3, 1; 2. 2, 1, 3; 3. 3, 2, 1; 4. 2, 3, 1

Page 70

1. Last; 2. First; 3. Next; 1. Next; 2. First; 3. Last

Pages 71–72

1. Get a bowl.; 2. Put two scoops of ice cream in the bowl.; 3. Squirt chocolate sauce over the ice cream.; 4. Pour sprinkles over the chocolate sauce.; 5. Add a cherry to the top.; 6. Eat the sundae.

Page 73

1. 1, 3, 2; 2. 2, 1, 3; 3. 2, 3, 1; 4. 3, 1, 2

Pages 74–75

4, 6, 1, 3, 2, 5

Page 76

1. A; 2. E; 3. F; 4. C; 5. B; 6. D

Answer Key

Page 77

Answers will vary.

Unit 5 Test

1. C; 2. C; 3. B; 4. D; 5. A; 6. C; 7. D; 8. A; 9. D; 10. D; 11. B; 12. C; 13. B; 14. D; 15. D; 16. A; 17. C; 18. B; 19. A; 20. C; Constructed response: First, I get into the car.; Then I put on my seat belt.; Next, my mom drives me to school.; Last, I get out of the car.

Page 85

Underline characters: Brain, Buster, Francine, Muffy, Becky, Rocky.

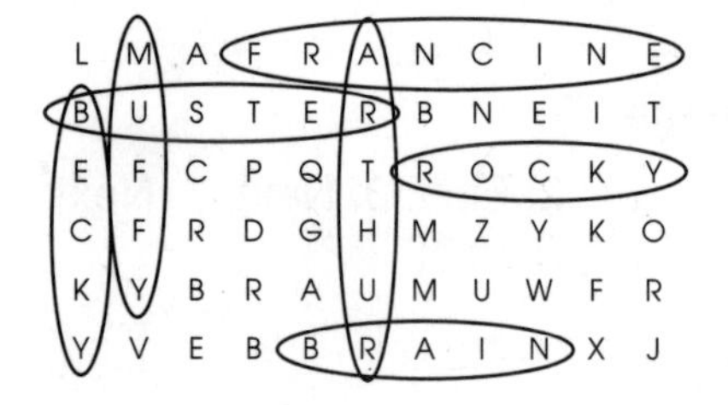

Page 86

1. Kip; 2. Sara; 3. Jack; 4. Ali

Page 87

1. funny; 2. afraid; 3. nice; 4. proud; 5. tired; 6. sad

Page 88

Kim: baseball, ice skate, sets the table; Kris: dance, sledding, sweeps the floor; Both: jump rope, swim, ride bikes

Page 89

1. C; 2. A; 3. D; 4. B

Page 90

a full moon

1. lake; 2. Afton; 3. June; 4. valley; 5. fall; 6. Mars; 7. boat; 8. zoo; 9. pond

Page 91

1. middle, beginning, end; 2. end, middle, beginning; 3. middle, end, beginning

Page 92

Exact wording may vary:
1. There were hundreds of ants on the blanket.; 2. The family moved to a picnic table to eat.; 3. Jackson could not find his black tennis shoes.; 4. He asked everyone in the family if they had seen his black shoes.

Pages 93–94

Answers will vary.

Unit 6 Test

1. A; 2. B; 3. A; 4. D; 5. D; 6. A; 7. B; 8. B; 9. C; 10. D; 11. D; 12. C; 13. D; 14. A; 15. A; 16. B; 17. C; 18. D; 19. A; 20. C; Constructed-response answers will vary.

Page 102

Answers will vary.

Pages 103–104

1. her hat and mittens; 2. Jan; 3. a snowman; 4. She fell down.; 5. hot chocolate

Page 105

Answers may vary. Possible answers include: 1. Go to the river.; 2. Mombo will win.; 3. The monkeys will take a nap.

Page 106

1. Kara is a girl.; 2. Flop is a rabbit.; 3. Mr. Grant is a teacher.

Page 107

1. B; 2. A; 3. B; 4. A; 5. B

Page 108

1. on a beach; 2. on a farm; 3. in a forest; 4. in a swimming pool

Page 109

Color blue: Earth is a planet.; Earth has a moon.; There are many stars in the sky.; The sun gives Earth light.

Unit 7 Test

1. A; 2. C; 3. D; 4. B; 5. C; 6. A; 7. D; 8. B; 9. C; 10. B; 11. C; 12. D; 13. A; 14. D; 15. C; Constructed-response answers will vary.

Final Review Test

1. C; 2. D; 3. A; 4. B; 5. C; 6. B; 7. A; 8. C; 9. C; 10. A; 11. B; 12. C; 13. A; 14. D; 15. C; 16. B; 17. D; 18. B; 19. A; 20. C; 21. D; 22. A; 23. C; 24. B; 25. D; 26. C; 27. D; 28. A; 29. B; 30. B; Constructed-response answers will vary.